Three Essays on Marxism

Three Essays on Marxism

Karl Korsch

Introduction by Paul Breines

Monthly Review Press
New York and London

Contents

Introduction
by Paul Breines

Korsch was born into a lower middle class family in Tostedt, a small town near Hamburg, on August 15, 1886.[1] He attended *Gymnasium* in Meiningen, near Thuringia, where his family had moved, and then studied at the universities of Munich, Berlin, Geneva, and Jena. With a "minor" in philosophy, Korsch received his doctorate of jurisprudence from Jena University in 1910. At Jena he also participated in the Free Student Movement which fought the influence of the fraternities and sought democratic and progressive reforms in the German educational system. In 1912, with a stipend from Jena, Korsch went to London to pursue post-doctoral studies. He was already a socialist, though not a member of the Social Democratic Party of Germany (SPD), and while in London he joined the Fabian Society. He also began to publish articles on political and social matters in the widely read German cultural review, *Die Tat* (The Deed).

1   For biographical information on Korsch, see: the essays by Fred Halliday and Paul Mattick cited in the bibliography appended to this introduction and Hermann Weber, *Die Wandlung des deutschen Kommunismus: Die Stalinisierung der KPD in der Weimarer Republik*, vol. 2 (Frankfurt-am-Main: Europäische Verlagsanstalt, 1969), pp. 192–93.

Key components of Korsch's later career appeared in outline during his association with the Fabians. For example, their focus on the idea of industrial democracy can be seen as the anticipation of his own subsequent preoccupation with the theory and practice of Workers' Councils, above all during the German Revolution of 1918–1919. Korsch was also impressed with the Fabians' "practical touch," which he favorably counterposed to the Germanic love for abstract theory and, more important, to the failure of most German socialists to elaborate positive socialist programs. While he would soon depart radically from the gradualism of the Fabian Society, this early concern for the practical and positive aspects of socialism characterized much of his later work.

Finally in this connection, Korsch was attracted by the Fabians' stress on the "will to socialism" and the "active socialist spirit" which, during these prewar years, he upheld against the philosophical determinism and evolutionism of the German Social Democrats. This motif might be called the embryo of Korsch's reconstruction of the "subjective factor" in Marxian theory as formulated in his later and best-known work, Marxism and Philosophy (1923).[2] On the other hand, it may be noted that Korsch was entirely at home with the aggressively positivist and antidialectical character of the Fabian outlook. How successfully he managed to extricate himself from this latter root remains a moot point.[3]

With the outbreak of World War I Korsch was recalled to Germany, where, since he had earlier completed officer training, he entered the German army as a lieutenant. He was, however, opposed to the war and for his outspokenness, as well as for his refusal to live in officers' quarters—he insisted on living with regular troops—he was demoted to corporal. Although he also refused to carry a gun, he saw front-line action and was twice hospitalized with serious wounds. In addition to being re-promoted to rank of lieutenant, Korsch received, among other medals for bravery, the vaunted Iron Cross, possession of which later helped him convince the German police to release him after his arrest as a subversive in 1933.

In 1917 Korsch joined the Independent Social Democratic Party (USPD) which had formed in that year as an antiwar split-off from the

---

2 Karl Korsch, Marxism and Philosophy, trans. Fred Halliday (New York: Monthly Review Press, 1971).
3 On the question of Korsch's positivism, see especially the essay by Mihály Vajda, cited in the bibliography.

SPD and which has accurately been referred to as a "quasi-revolutionary party." At the beginning of the German Revolution in November 1918, Korsch himself was a quasi-revolutionary, as reflected in his participation in the new republican government's Socialization Commission on the one hand, and his participation in a revolutionary soldiers' council on the other. Throughout 1919, however, Korsch moved to the left, although the Revolution did not. Still in the USPD, he became a leading theorist of the Berlin Workers' Councils and Revolutionary Shop Stewards grouped around Richard Müller, Ernst Däumig, and the journal, *Der Arbeiter-Rat* (The Workers' Council).[4]

In the spring and summer of 1919, under the impact of revolutionary motion and aided by the influence of a long-since-forgotten academic socialist, Robert Wilbrandt, Korsch threw himself into feverish study of Marx and Engels. He began to think and write as a Marxist and became more critical than ever of the "official" Marxism of the Social Democrats. He defined his outlook at this stage with the term "practical socialism." The actual roots, at least of the term itself, go back to the early years of the Fabian Society, although Korsch was re-casting its meaning in a revolutionary mold.

In 1920, with the split in the USPD—masterminded in part by the Moscow Executive of the Communist International—Korsch went with the left wing into the Communist Party of Germany (KPD). In spite of his concern that Lenin's Twenty-one Points—conditions for membership in the Communist International—implied Russian domination of the European sections, he viewed the KPD as the only viable organizational alternative to Social Democratic reformism and treachery. It should also be stressed that, while Korsch had now become a "Leninist," Leninism for him and not a few others at the time did not primarily mean the theory of the vanguard party as the agent of revolution but, rather, revolutionary activism on all fronts of the class struggle. It was not long before this conception of Leninism put Korsch—and others—in conflict with the Leninists.

His intellectual talents and close contacts with militants in Berlin and Jena factories enabled Korsch to emerge, during 1921 and 1922, as an influential theorist and functionary in the KPD. Active in the party's

---

4 Discussions of Korsch's role in the Workers' Councils movement in the German Revolution can be found in Peter von Oertzen, *Betriebsräte in der Novemberrevolution* (Düsseldorf: Droste, 1963), p. 242f; and in Dieter Schneider and Rudolf Kuda, eds., *Arbeiterräte in der Novemberrevolution: Ideen, Wirkungen, Dokumente* (Frankfurt-am-Main: Suhrkamp, 1968).

press offices, Korsch was primarily engaged in the Educational Section, preparing and teaching courses for workers in the fundamentals of Marxism. In addition to several booklets intended for use in these courses, in 1922 Korsch published his *Arbeitsrecht für Betriebsräte* (Labor Law for Factory Councils), a Marxist critique of bourgeois labor law and an extensive blueprint for its proletarian replacement.

The year 1923 was decisive for Korsch and for German Communism. October 1923 saw the incoherent attempt at revolutionary seizure of power by the KPD in Thuringia and Saxony. Quickly quashed by government troops and resulting in the departure of nearly half the KPD membership, the "German October" sounded the death knell, for those who had not heard it earlier, of the "revolution across Europe." Although Korsch was critical of the party's "united front from above" tactic, he served, on order, as Minister of Justice in the short-lived "workers' government" set up by the KPD and SPD in Thuringia. He was also promoted to the rank of full professor at Jena University. More important in retrospect, 1923 was the year of the publication of Korsch's essay, "Marxism and Philosophy" (published later in the year in book form), which was quickly to join Georg Lukács' *History and Class Consciousness* as one of the most controversial theoretical texts of the European Marxist movement.

Early in 1924 Korsch became a Communist delegate to the Thuringian Landtag and in July of that year a Communist deputy to the Reichstag. Following the October 1923 disaster, he moved into the KPD's left wing which initiated, with backing from Stalin and Zinoviev, a purge of the Right. In this connection, Korsch was made editor of the KPD's theoretical organ, *Die Internationale*. The real significance of these developments was not clear to the German participants. What appeared to be a revolutionary cleansing of the party was in fact the start of a process which, in E. H. Carr's words, destroyed "the large measure of independence hitherto enjoyed by the KPD" and turned it "into a sparring ground for Russian factional disputes."[5]

The KPD left wing was the vehicle of this process, the so-called Bolshevization of the sections of the Communist International, although the real Leftists, Korsch among them, were soon to be its victims. So, for example, at the Fifth World Congress of the Comintern held in Moscow in the summer of 1924—Korsch was a KPD delegate—Zinoviev

5   E. H. Carr, *The Interregnum, 1923–1924* (Baltimore: Penguin Books, 1969) p. 251.

denounced *Marxism and Philosophy* along with Lukács' *History and Class Consciousness* as idealist and ultra-left deviations from Marxism-Leninism. The reservations Korsch had suspended on joining the KPD in 1920 were, if belatedly, proving well-founded: Russian domination of the European revolutionary movement was taking clear shape. Korsch's view of the matter was succinctly summarized when, in the midst of a speech by Bukharin outlining the need for the European parties to adopt a new "united front" in the face of the "temporary stabilization" of world capital, he cried out from the floor: "Soviet imperialism!"[6]

Early in 1925 Korsch was removed from editorship of *Die Internationale* as an ultra-leftist, the party faction whose leading theorist he had indeed become. Faced on the one hand with a systematic campaign against it led by the Comintern Executive and, on the other, by incessant internal splintering, the ultra-left was virtually decimated within a year. In April 1926 on the Reichstag floor, Korsch, recalling Rosa Luxemburg's warnings against an alliance between Russian and Prussian militarism, denounced a pending arms pact between the Soviet and German governments and condemned the Comintern as a counter-revolutionary force. The KPD then demanded that he give up his Reichstag seat or be expelled from the party. He refused to give up his seat, which he held until 1928, and was promptly expelled from the KPD at the end of April.

A diminishing group of comrades gathered around Korsch and an irregular publication, *Kommunistische Politik*. Calling itself the "decisive Left" this group, as Hermann Weber reports, vanished from the historical stage by early 1928.[7] By that time, with the completion of the Stalinization of the Communist movement and with his basic differences with Trotskyism on the question of the Soviet Union, Korsch became a free-floating Marxist theorist. For a time he led a discussion circle in Berlin in "critical Marxism," which included among its participants Bertolt Brecht and the novelist Alfred Döblin. Beginning roughly in 1929 Korsch initiated a major re-evaluation of Marxism which was to occupy him through the rest of his career. This project essentially con-

---

6 Gustav Hilger, *The Incompatible Allies: A Memoir-History of German–Soviet Relations, 1918–1941* (New York: Houghton-Mifflin, 1953), p. 108.
7 Weber, *Die Wandlung*, p. 193. The best treatment of the story of the German ultra-left in the mid-1920s is Siegfried Bahne, "Zwischen 'Luxemburgismus' und 'Stalinismus': Die 'Ultralinke' Opposition in der KPD," *Vierteljahrshefte für Zeitgeschichte*, vol. IX, no. 4 (October 1961), pp. 359–83.

sisted of a critique of both Kautskyism and Leninism on the one hand, and an attempt to elaborate a self-critical and genuinely proletarian Marxism on the other. The essays gathered in this volume are among the results of this latter effort.[8]

In 1933, with the Nazi seizure of power, Korsch fled to Denmark, where he began his close friendship with Brecht. Two years later he went to England and in 1936 to the United States, where he was to remain until his death in 1961. In the mid-1930s Korsch had loose contacts with the emigré Frankfurt School in whose journal he published several reviews. During the 1940s he wrote often in the publications of the anti-Leninist "Council Communists" (*Living Marxism, New Essays*) grouped around Paul Mattick and Anton Pannekoek. Although linked to circles such as these and often working closely with such friends as the behavioral psychologist Kurt Lewin, politically Korsch was alone during the last two and a half decades of his life. In the early and mid-1950s he made brief visits to Germany, where he addressed several trade union groups. Korsch was, however, already beginning to suffer from what was to be a fatal brain illness. He died in Belmont, Massachusetts, on October 21, 1961.

Bibliography of Some Recent Commentaries on Korsch

alternative. April 1965. This number of the Marxist literary journal published in West Berlin is devoted to the theme, "Karl Korsch: Lehrer Bertolt Brechts" (Karl Korsch: Bertolt Brecht's Teacher). It contains selections from Korsch's unpublished papers, including correspondence with Brecht; useful biographical and bibliographical data; and brief editorial comments on Korsch's work.

Breines, Paul. Review of Giuseppe Vacca, *Lukács O Korsch?* Telos, Spring 1970, pp. 215–20.

Cerutti, Furio. "Hegel, Lukács, Korsch. Zum dialektischen Selbstverständnis des kritischen Marxismus" (Hegel, Lukács, Korsch:

8 The major results of Korsch's project are: *Die materialistische Geschichtsauffassung. Eine Auseinandersetzung mit Karl Kautsky* (Leipzig: L. Hirschfeld, 1929), a critique of Kautsky; "The Present State of the Problem of 'Marxism and Philosophy,' " which is the preface to the second edition (1930) of *Marxism and Philosophy* and which has been reprinted in all subsequent editions—it is a critique of Kautsky and Lenin and the bonds between them; *Karl Marx* (London: Chapman and Hall, 1938), a book which contains a greatly expanded treatment of the themes presented in the essays in this volume.

Toward a dialectical self-analysis of critical Marxism). In *Aktualität und Folgen der Philosophie Hegels*, edited by Oskar Negt, pp. 195–210. Frankfurt-am-Main: Suhrkamp, 1970. A concise and brilliant essay which, however, deals primarily with Lukács.

Fetscher, Iring. *Karl Marx and Marxism*. New York: Herder and Herder, 1971. See especially the chapter, "The Relation of Marxism to Hegel." An essay originally published in 1958 in the journal *Marxismusstudien*, this is one of the seminal post-World War II reinterpretations of Marxism from the standpoint of Lukács' and Korsch's work of the early 1920s; as such it played an important role in the revival of Korsch in Germany.

Gabel, Joseph. "Korsch, Lukács et le probleme de la conscience de classe." *Annales*, May–June 1966, pp. 668–80. The discussion of Korsch places the struggle against dogmatism at the center of his work.

Gerlach, Erich. "Die Entwicklung des Marxismus von der revolutionären Philosophie zur wissenschaftlichen Theorie proletarischen Handelns bei Karl Korsch" (The Development of Marxism from Revolutionary Philosophy to a Scientific Theory of Proletarian Action in the Work of Karl Korsch). Introduction to *Marxismus und Philosophie*, by Karl Korsch. Frankfurt-am-Main: Europäische Verlagsanstalt, 1966.

—. "Karl Korsch's Undogmatic Marxism." *International Socialism*, Winter 1964–65, pp. 22–27. Both of Gerlach's essays are extremely useful philologically, although the author, a "left" Social Democrat in West Germany, reads Korsch as a forerunner of present-day nonrevolutionary "structural reform" theory.

Halliday, Fred. "Karl Korsch: An Introduction." Introduction to *Marxism and Philosophy*, by Karl Korsch. Translated by Fred Halliday. New York: Monthly Review Press, 1971. A useful capsule intellectual-political biography which takes Korsch to task for having failed sufficiently to adopt the Leninist theory of the vanguard and armed insurrection.

Mattick, Paul. "The Marxism of Karl Korsch." *Survey*, October 1964, pp. 86–97. A fine essay by the man who stood at the center of the emigré "Council Communist" groups with which Korsch was associated during the 1940s and 1950s.

Politikon. October–November 1971. This number of the independent, left-wing student magazine published in Göttingen is devoted to Korsch. It contains new essays by Oskar Negt, Giuseppe Vacca, and

Gian Enrico Rusconi, other works by whom are cited in this bibliography. The magazine's editors place Korsch in the context of, on the one hand, contemporary "cultural revolution" and, on the other, their own opposition to resurgent Marxism-Leninism.

Rusconi, Gian Enrico. "Karl Korsch e la strategia consiliare-sindicale" (Karl Korsch and the Strategy of Workers' Councils). *Problemi del Socialismo*, no. 41, 1969: pp. 762–77. A high-level review essay of Korsch's book, *Arbeitsrecht für Betriebsräte* (Labor Law for Factory Councils [1922]).

—. *La teoria critica della società*. Bologna: il Mulino, 1968. A solid and perceptive book tracing the "critical theory of society" from Lukács and Korsch through the Frankfurt School and Marcuse's recent work. Chapter 2 deals with Korsch's *Marxism and Philosophy*; chapter 5 with his *Karl Marx*.

Schneider, Dieter, and Rudolf Kuda, eds. *Arbeiterräte in der November-revolution: Ideen, Wirkungen, Dokumente* (Workers' Councils in the November Revolution: Ideas, Impact, Documents). Frankfurt-am-Main: Suhrkamp, 1968. Korsch's role as a leading theorist-activist in the Workers' Councils in the German Revolution looms large in the editors' introduction.

Vacca, Giuseppe. *Lukács O Korsch?* (Lukács or Korsch?). Bari: de Donato, 1969. Important as the first attempt systematically to *distinguish between* Korsch's and Lukács' perspectives. Vacca takes Korsch over Lukács and views the former's *Karl Marx* (1938) as seminal for a contemporary reconstruction of Marxism.

Vajda, Mihály. "Karl Korsch: Marxism and Philosophy." In *The Unknown Dimension: European Marxism Since Lenin*, edited by Dick Howard and Karl E. Klare, pp. 131–46. New York: Basic Books, 1972. A provocative, fraternal polemic with Korsch's *Marxism and Philosophy* by one of the associates of the Budapest School of Marxism whose guiding figure, until his recent death, was Georg Lukács. Vajda traces what he deems key flaws in Korsch's work to the latter's failure to appropriate and develop Hegel's and Marx's conceptions of labor and "objectivation."

Leading Principles of Marxism: a Restatement

Marxism versus Sociology

WHAT IS the relationship between Marxism and modern sociological teaching? If we think of the sociology originated by Comte, and first named by him, as a special section in the system of constituted sciences, we shall find no link between it and Marxism. Marx and Engels paid no attention to either the name or content of this ostensibly new branch of knowledge. When Marx felt himself compelled to take terse notice of Comte's *Cours de Philosophie Positive*, thirty years after its appearance, 'because the English and French make such a fuss about the fellow', he still spoke of 'Positivism' and 'Comtism' as of something to which he was 'thoroughly opposed as a politician' and of which he had 'a very poor opinion as a man of science'.[1] Marx's attitude is theoretically and historically well-founded. The science of socialism, as

* Originally published in English in *Marxist Quarterly* (published by the American Marxist Association), Vol 1/3, Oct-Dec 1937, pp 356-378.

1 See Marx's letter to Engels of 7/7/66, *Marx-Engels-Gesamt Ausgabe* (MEGA III, 3; p 345); also Marx's letter to Beesly of 12/6/71, and further

formulated by Marx, owed nothing to this 'sociology' of the nineteenth and twentieth centuries which originated with Comte and was propagated by Mill and Spencer. It would be more correct to say that 'sociology' is a reaction against modern socialism. From this standpoint only is it possible to understand the essential unity of the diverse theoretical and practical tendencies which during the last hundred years have found their expression in this science. As with Comte in his relation to St. Simon, his 'great master',[2] so have the latter bourgeois 'sociologists' opposed another way of answering the questions first raised by the rising proletarian movement to the theory and thus also to the practice of *socialism*. To these issues, which modern historical development has put on the agenda of present-day society, Marxism stands in a much more original and direct relationship than the whole of the so-called 'sociology' of Comte, Spencer and their followers. Fundamentally, then, there exists no theoretical relationship between those two doctrines of society. Bourgeois sociologists refer to the revolutionary socialist science of the proletariat as 'an unscientific mixture of theory and politics'. Socialists, on the other hand, dismiss bourgeois sociology as mere 'ideology'.

The position of Marx, however, is quite different toward the first 'Enquirers into the Social Nature of Man', who in the preceding centuries, in the radical struggles of the rising bourgeois class against the obsolete feudal order, had first set up the new idea of *Civil Society* as a revolutionary slogan, and had even unearthed, in the new science of *Political Economy*, the material foundations of this new 'civilised' form of society.[3]

According to Marx's own statement, made in 1859, in the preface to his *Contribution to the Critique of Political Economy*,[4] he had

the letter to Engels of 23/5/69 in which Spencer's name is curtly mentioned along with some other contemporary writers (M E G A I I I, 4; p 58). See also the ironical dismissal of 'Comtist recipes for the cook-shops of the future' in Marx's reply to the reviewer of *Capital* in the Paris *Revue positiviste* in the preface to the second edition of *Capital*, 1872-73, and Engels' letter to Tönnies of 24/1/95 quoted in G. Mayer's Biography of Friedrich Engels (1934) Vol I I, p 552. Letters of 7/7/66 and 12/6/71 in Marx-Engels, *Selected Correspondence*, Moscow nd, pp 217-8, 322.

2   See Levy-Bruehl, *La Philosophie d'Auguste Comte* (1900), p 8.

3   See, for example, Adam Ferguson, *An Essay on the History of Civil Society*, 1767 and Adam Smith, *An Inquiry into the Nature and Causes of the Wealth of Nations*, 1776.

4   Hereafter referred to as *Preface 1859*. In English in Marx-Engels *Selected Works* (1 vol ed), London 1968, pp 181-5.

begun the development of his materialistic theory of society sixteen years earlier with a critical revision of Hegel's *Philosophy of Law*. This was a task he had set himself because of certain grave doubts which had recently assailed him in regard to his Hegelian idealistic creed. Previously, as an editor of the *Rheinische Zeitung* (1842-43), he had for the first time found himself called upon to discuss 'so-called material interests'. He had already begun to study 'economic questions' and had become vaguely acquainted·with the ideas of 'French Socialism and Communism'. His criticism of Hegel led him to the conclusion that 'legal relations as well as forms of state cannot be understood out of themselves nor out of the so-called general development of the human mind, but on the contrary, are rooted in the material conditions of life, the aggregate of which Hegel, following the precedent of the English and French of the eighteenth century, grouped together under the name of "civil society" – and that the anatomy of civil society is to be sought in political economy.'

We see here the decisive significance which the notion of 'civil society' had gained for the young Marx who was at that time just completing his transition from Hegelian idealism to his later materialistic theory. While still formally basing his materialistic criticism of Hegel's idealistic glorification of the state on the realistic conclusions (unexpected in an idealist philosopher) regarding the nature of civil society which he had found embodied in Hegel's *Philosophy of Law*,[5] Marx now definitely abandoned Hegel and all his idealistic philosophy. Instead he associated himself with those earlier investigators into the nature of society who had arisen in the period of revolutionary development of the English and French bourgeoisie, when the name 'sociology' had not yet been invented, but 'society' had already been discovered as a special and independent realm of knowledge.

Hegel, indeed, had not derived that deep realistic knowledge of 'civil society', which stands in such sharp relief to the rest of his book,[6] from an independent study of the then extremely backward state of German society. He took both the name and content of his 'civil society' ready-made from the French and English social philosophers, politicians and economists. Behind Hegel, as Marx said, stand

5 See the comprehensive manuscripts of 1843 now published in M E G A I, 1, 1; pp 401-553. qv Marx, *Critique of Hegel's Philosophy of Right*, Cambridge 1970.

6 See Hegel, *Philosophy of Law*, Part III, Section 2 (Civil Society), esp §188 et seq (System of Needs), §230 et seq (Police).

the 'English and French of the eighteenth century' with their new discoveries of the structure and movement of society, who in their turn
reflect the real historical development which culminated in the Industrial Revolution in England after the middle of the eighteenth century and in the great French Revolution of 1789 to 1815.

Marx, then, in developing his new socialist and proletarian
science, took his cue from that early study of society, which, although
it was first communicated to him by Hegel, had really been born in
the revolutionary epoch of the bourgeoisie. In the first place he took
over the results of 'classical political economy' (from Petty and
Boisguillebert through Quesnay and Smith up to Ricardo) consciously
developing them as that which the great bourgeois investigators had
already more or less unconsciously taken them to be, ie the basic
structure or, as it were, 'the skeleton' of civil society. Even this basic
importance of political economy, to which Marx alludes in calling it
the 'anatomy of civil society', had before him been recognised by his
immediate predecessors, the German idealist philosophers, Kant,
Fichte and Hegel. In the philosophical system of Hegel, 'civil society'
is based on the 'system of needs' explored by the new science of political economy, and the philosopher had, in an earlier work, even expressly described the 'system of needs' as the 'first form of government',
as opposed to such higher developed forms as the state and the law.

The very pungency with which Marx in his later writings repeatedly emphasised that post-classical bourgeois economy (the so-
called 'vulgar economy') had not advanced beyond Ricardo in any
important points,[7] and scornfully dismissed the new socio-scientific
synthesis of Comte's Positivism for the infinitely greater achievement
of Hegel,[8] only shows once more the lasting influence of that early
phase of economic and social thought on the theory of Marx. This is
true even though his analysis of the new development of society and the
new needs and aims of the proletariat, now emerging as an independent
class, far transcended the results of those older theories. The proletarian class guided by the Marxist theory is therefore not only, as
Friedrich Engels put it, 'the inheritor of German classical philosophy',[9]

7   See *Capital* I, Moscow 1959, p 80 footnote 2 and *Theories of Surplus
Value* III, pp 571-76 (German ed).

8   See letter to Engels of 7/7/66.

9   See the concluding sentence of *Ludwig Feuerbach and the End of Classical Philosophy*, 1888. A similar statement, with an amplifying reference to the

it also is the inheritor of classical political economy and social research. As such it has transformed the traditional classical theory in accordance with the changes in historical conditions.

Marx no longer regards bourgeois society from the standpoint of its first phase of development and its opposition to the feudal structure of medieval society. He is not only interested in the static laws of its existence. He treats bourgeois society as historical in all its traits and therefore merely a transitory organisation of society. He explores the whole process of its historical genesis and development, and the inherent tendencies which, in their further development, lead to its revolutionary overthrow. He finds these tendencies twofold: *objective* in the economic basis of bourgeois society, *subjective* in the new division of social classes arising out of this same economic basis and not out of politics, law, ethics, etc. Thus civil society, which until then had constituted a homogeneous whole, opposed only to feudalism, is now torn into two opposed 'parties'. The assumed 'civil society' is in reality 'bourgeois society', ie a society based on the cleavage of classes, in which the bourgeois class controls other classes economically and therefore politically and culturally. So at last *la classe la plus laborieuse et la plus misérable* enters the widened horizon of social science. Marxist theory recognises the class war of the oppressed and exploited wage labourers of present-day society to be a war for the supersession of the present structure of society by a more highly developed form of society. As a materialistic science of the contemporary development of bourgeois society, Marxist theory is at the same time a practical instrument for the struggle of the proletariat to bring about the realisation of proletarian society.

The later artificial detachment of sociology as a special branch of learning, whose scientific origin dates from Comte, and, at the best, allows the great original thinkers who have done the real productive work in this field to stand as its 'forerunners', represents nothing more than an escape from the practical and, therefore, also theoretical tasks of the present historical epoch. Marx's new socialist and proletarian science, which further developed the revolutionary theory of the classical founders of the doctrine of society in a way corresponding to the changed historical situation, is the genuine social science of our time.

equal importance of the 'developed economic and political conditions in England and France', is found in the preface to the first German edition of Engels' *Socialism, Utopian and Scientific*, 1882.

The Principle of Historical Specification

Marx comprehends all things social in terms of a definite historical epoch. He criticises all the categories of the bourgeois theorists of society in which this specific character has been effaced. Already in his first economic work we find him reproaching Ricardo for having applied the specifically bourgeois concept of *rent* to 'landed property of all epochs and of all countries. This is the error of all economists who represent bourgeois production relations as eternal.' [10]

The scope of the principle of historical specification is clearly demonstrated in this example. *Landed property* has been widely different in character and has played very different roles in the various historical epochs of society. Already the different ways in which primitive communal property in land had been broken up, directly influenced the varied forms of the later development of society based upon private property.[11] Up to the middle ages *landed property* (agriculture) constituted, according to Marx, the central category, dominating all the other categories of production, just as *capital* does in present-day bourgeois society.[12] The different ways in which, in different countries, after the victory of the capitalist mode of production, feudal property in land was subjected to capital; the different ways in which rent was transformed into a part of capitalist surplus value, and agriculture into an industry – all retain their importance for the capitalist systems which arose therefrom, for the different forms of the labour movement which subsequently developed within them, and for the different forms in which the transition to the socialist mode of production will ultimately be effected in each of the different systems. For this reason Marx investigated with particular care, to the end of his life, the history of landed property and rent as shown on the one hand in the *United States*, and on the other hand in *Russia*. In the same way, at the end of the nineteenth century, Lenin, in his *Development of Capitalism in Russia*, analysed particularly the specific historical forms of

10   See *Poverty of Philosophy*, Moscow nd, p 154.

11   See *Contribution to the Critique of Political Economy*, 1859, translated by N I Stone, Charles Kerr, Chicago 1904, p 29 footnote 1.

12   See the ms of a 'general introduction' to the *Critique of Political Economy* dated 25/8/57, first printed in *Neue Zeit* XXI, 1, 1903 – hereafter referred to as *Introduction* 1857. Available in English in Stone translation (note 11 above) and in C J Arthur's edition of Marx-Engels, *The German Ideology*, London 1970, pp 124-152. Page references are to the Arthur edition.

this transition process.[13] Yet all this comprehensive study of the various historical forms serves, with both Marx and Lenin, only as a base for the working out of the specific character of *capitalist* rent in fully developed *bourgeois society.*

In the fundamental analysis of the modern capitalist mode of production, which forms the subject matter of the first book of *Capital,* Marx does not deal with the category of rent at all. What is discussed there, in addition to the general function of the soil as an element of the labour process itself,[14] is only the different ways by which the transition to the modern capitalist mode of production reacted upon the conditions of the agricultural proletariat, first, in developed capitalist countries,[15] second, in such countries as Ireland that had fallen behind in the process of industrialization, and finally in the colonia' countries.[16]

Marx discusses 'rent' in the proper place, in a section of the third book of *Capital,* in which the special forms of capitalist *distribution* are analysed as they arise from the special historical forms of capitalist *production.*[17] Even here, there is no room for an independent exposition of earlier historical forms. Only a few scattered remarks throw a flash of light on the contrast between the modern bourgeois form of landed property and past historical forms; and only an additional closing chapter – and indeed, of that only a part – is devoted to the historical *Genesis of Capitalist Rent.*[18] Indeed, as Marx says in the opening phrase of this whole section, 'the analysis of landed property in its various historical forms lies beyond the scope of this work'.[19]

The concept of 'rent', then, as discussed in the Marxist theory, is in no way a general term referring to landed property of all epochs. The form of landed property which is considered in *Capital* is 'a specifically historical one; it is that form into which feudal land ownership and small peasants' agriculture have been *transformed* through the in-

---

13   Lenin began to write this book in 1896 while he was in prison and went on with it during his exile in Siberia. The first Russian edition appeared in 1899, the second in 1907. English edition in *Collected Works* III.

14   See *Capital* I, pp 178 et seq.

15   *ibid,* pp 639 et seq; *ibid,* pp 664 et seq.

16   *ibid,* chapters 32 and 33 dealing with 'so-called original accumulation' and the 'modern colonial system'.

17   See *Capital* III, Moscow edition, pp 614-812.

18   *ibid,* pp 782-812.

19   *ibid,* p 614.

fluence of capital and of the capitalist mode of production'.[20] In this
sense, and in this sense only, an analysis of modern capitalist rent, or
of that portion of the surplus value produced by industrial capital
which falls into the hands of the capitalistic landowner, is a necessary
part of the complete analysis of the process of capitalist production
which is embodied in the three books of *Capital*.

The application of the principle of historical specification is
further demonstrated by the way Marx deals with the different historical forms of capital itself. Just as in the present epoch *industrial capital* appears as the standard form, so did *merchants' capital* and its twin
brother, *interest-bearing capital*, and the various sub-forms of these
(more exactly described by Marx as 'capital for trading in goods',
'capital for trading in money', 'capital for lending money') occupy an
independent and, in certain respects, a predominating position in the
epochs preceding capitalist society, and, indeed, in the first phases of
capitalist society itself. Even in present-day fully developed capitalist
economy the merchant and the banker, though not involved in actual
production like the industrial capitalist, still perform a definite function in the circulation of capital. They also participate in the distribution of the total 'surplus value', a considerable part of the yearly
amount at the disposal of the capitalist class falls to their share as
'commercial profit' and 'interest' – just as we have seen another part of
it going in the form of 'rent' to landed owners of property who have
as little to do with actual production. Moneylenders' capital has even
recaptured an important position – though not, as many Marxists have
believed, a definite supremacy – in its new form as an integral part of
the modern so-called 'finance capital', ie a system of highly concen-
trated capital created by the fusion of private and state-controlled bank
capital with trust and state-controlled industrial capital.[21]

The Marxist analysis of modern capitalist production starts from
the assumption that the previously independent forms of trading-
capital and money-capital have been *transformed* into mere accessor-
ies of the new prevailing form. It is true that capitalist production
even today bears the stamp of its historical origin – the intrusion of the
merchant into the sphere of feudal production. All capitalist production remains essentially a *production for sale*. Every article resulting

20   *ibid*, pp 614 et seq.

21   See Hilferding's *Finance Capital*, 1910 and Lenin's *Imperialism, the
Newest Stage of Capitalism*, 1917.

from capitalist production is to be sold as a commodity, whether it is sold to another industrial capitalist who needs it for carrying on his own process of production or, ultimately, to the immediate consumer. Again the very way in which 'capital' first arose and gained control of production in the shape of *money*, as supplied by wealthy individuals, merchants, usurers, etc, constantly repeats itself under the present condition of fully developed capitalist production. Every new aggregate of capital, even today, 'enters upon the stage, ie comes into the market – the commodity market, the labour market or the money market – still in the form of money that by a definite process has to be transformed into capital'.[22]

Nevertheless the 'secret', not only of 'how capital produces' but also of 'how capital *is* produced' – and incidentally the key to the abolition of all capitalist exploitation and wage-slavery – can in no way be theoretically discovered by an analysis of the functions performed by those 'accessory' forms of capital in the process of circulation, or of the revenues which accrue to the capitalists concerned, in consideration of the 'services' they perform in this sphere. 'One will therefore understand,' says Marx, 'why in our analysis of the basic form of capital, of the form in which it determines the economic organisation of modern society, its popular, and as it were, antediluvian forms, "trading capital" and "usurers capital", are for the present (viz in the analysis of the actual process of capitalist production in the first book of *Capital*) entirely ignored.' [23]

Even when, in the second and third books of *Capital*, Marx comes back to these 'antediluvian forms' in his analysis of capitalist circulation and distribution,[24] he takes as his main theme, not their historical development, but only the specific form into which they have been transformed by the action of modern industrial capital. Just as with rent, the historical analyses which run through the whole of Marx's work, and both the concluding chapters added to the sections concerned, under the headings *Historical data concerning merchants' capital* and *Pre-capitalistic conditions*,[25] merely serve to illuminate that great historical process through which, in the course of centuries and

22   See *Capital* I, p 146, and for a more detailed analysis of the various forms which capital assumes in its different stages, *Capital* II, Chap 1.

23   See *Capital* I, p 163.

24   See *Capital* II, Chapters 1-4; III, Chapters 16-20, 21-36.

25   *ibid*, III, Chapters 20 and 36.

millenia, *trade* and *money transactions* lost more and more of their originally dominating position until they assumed their present place as mere detached and one-sidedly developed modes of existence of the various functions which industrial capital sometimes adopts and sometimes discards within the sphere of its circulation.

There is one aspect alone, under which rent as well as trading-capital and money-capital might have been treated as a proper subject in Marx's analysis of the modern capitalist mode of production and of the economic form of society based thereon. According to an original and more comprehensive plan, Marx would have followed up the discussion of the more strictly economic questions of production, circulation and distribution, social classes etc, as contained in the three books of *Capital*, by an investigation of what may be called 'economic questions of an higher order' such as the relation between *town and country* and the *international relations of production*.[26]

Only with these later researches would Marx's analysis have reached the point where the antagonism of landed property to *capital*, as well as that of trade and money-capital to *industrial capital* survives in present-day society; the former as a relation between agricultural and town industry and as an international relation between primarily agrarian and industrial countries – the latter as a relation between trading cities and factory towns, and on an international scale between commercial and industrial states.

The principle of historical specification as illustrated by the preceding examples (landed property and the various forms of capital) is strictly adhered to by Marx in all his economic and socio-historical researches. He deals with all categories in that specific form and in that specific connection in which they appear in modern bourgeois society.[27]

The contrast which exists in this respect between Marx and his forerunners, comes out most strikingly in a comparison. While the work of the last representative of classical bourgeois economy, David Ricardo, is devoted to the *Principles of Political Economy*, Marx strictly limited his economic research to 'modern bourgeois production',[28] and finally

26   See *Introduction* 1857, p 148 and *Capital* I, p 352 where Marx expressly states that he cannot here go further into the topic of the cleavage between town and country, although 'the whole economic history of society is summed up in the movement of this antagonism'. – See also the more detailed discussion of the later changes in the plan of *Capital* in the introduction to my edition, Berlin 1932, pp 8 et seq (reprinted in this collection of essays).

27   See *Introduction* 1857, pp 140 et seq.

28   *ibid*, p 125.

gave the work which contains the whole of his analysis and critique of all traditional political economy the plain and definite name *Capital*. Ricardo begins the exposition of his system with the general concept of 'value'; Marx commences his critical investigation of the theory and the facts underlying modern bourgeois economy with the analysis of an external object, a palpable thing – 'commodity'. Again, Ricardo frees the traditional economic concept of value from the last earthly impurities that were still attached to it by his predecessors; while Marx, on the contrary, regards even the concept of 'commodity' in its isolation, as it applies also to conditions other than those of present-day bourgeois production, as too abstract a category, and defines it specifically as an element of 'bourgeois wealth' [29] or as the 'wealth of those societies in which the capitalist mode of production prevails'.[30] Only in this specific definition does 'commodity' form the subject matter of his investigation. Only as properties of such a commodity do the general concepts of 'value in use' and 'value in exchange', and the other terms of the classical economic system derived from these fundamental concepts, interest him. He does not treat them as eternal categories. Nor does he for that matter transform himself into an historian. While fully aware of the fact that many economic categories of modern bourgeois society occurred, in other specific relations to the whole of the mode of production, also in earlier epochs, he does not go into the history of 'money', of 'exchange of commodities', of 'wage-labour', or that of 'co-operation', 'division of labour', etc. He discusses the different stages of the historical development of all these economic concepts only in so far as it is necessary for his main theme: the analysis of the specific character assumed by them in modern bourgeois society.

All the economic terms of Marx, then, as opposed to those of the classical bourgeois economists, refer to a specific historical epoch of production. This applies even to that, most general term, *value*, which, according to Marx, must still be distinguished from 'value in exchange' – the latter being only the external form in which the intrinsic 'value' of a given commodity manifests itself in the ratio of exchange of such commodities.[31] This most abstract term, which Marx adopted from the later classical economists, has been highly suspect to some well-meaning but superficial interpreters of Marx who found that the

29   See *Contribution to the Critique of Political Economy*, opening sentence.

30   See *Capital* I, opening sentence.

31   See *Capital* I, pp 36-38.

concept of an intrinsic 'value', distinct from exchange-value, reeks of
scholasticism, metaphysical realism, Hegelian idealism and what not,
and for this reason does no credit to a 'materialistic' science. As a
matter of fact, Marx discussed just these fundamental concepts of his
economic theory in a somewhat obscure language, thereby avowedly
'coquetting' with the 'modes of expression peculiar to that mighty
thinker, the idealist philosopher Hegel'.[32] However, there is no point
in accepting the term exchange-value, as taken by Marx from his forerunners, the founders of classical political economy, and rejecting that
of intrinsic 'value' which was used by Marx only as a means to work
out more clearly the true content of the 'value' concept of the classical
writers and to expose critically what he called the 'fetishism' underlying the whole of their economic theory.[33]

Marx was fully conscious of the fact that all concepts of 'value'
are strictly relative terms. They either denote an immediate relation
between objects and man (which becomes a reality by actual use or
consumption), or a relation of a different order (realised by the exchange of such objects), viz the quantitative relation in which use-
values of one sort are exchanged for those of another sort whenever
they are exchanged. The relations of the latter order had been regarded
by the later classical economists as the only 'value' to be dealt with in
a strictly economic science, and had been styled by them *value in
exchange* or *value* proper, as distinguished from mere utility or *'use-
value'*. Marx easily agreed with the classical writers when they established the difference in kind prevailing between *value* as a quantitative
relation arising through the exchange of commodities, ie by a social
process; and *use-value* as a merely qualitative relation between external objects and man. But he did not agree with them in the ultimate location of the social relations manifesting themselves in the
'value' relations of the commodities as established by their exchange.
A closer investigation of the economic concept of 'value' shows that
this concept expresses a relation arising not between the commodities
as exchanged on the market, but rather a relation previously established
between human beings co-operating in the production of such commodities, *a social relation of production arising between man and man.*
Indeed, the main result of Marx's criticism of the traditional theory of
political economy consists in the discovery and description of these

32   See postscript to second edition of *Capital*, 1872-73 – hereafter referred
to as *Postscript* 1873. In Moscow edition, pp 12-20.

33   See *Capital* I, pp 71-83.

fundamental social relations of men – relations which, for a definite historical epoch, appear to the subjects concerned in the disguised and, as it were, perverted form of relations of things, viz as 'value-relations' of the commodities co-operatively produced by them and mutually exchanged on the market.

'Value', then, in all its denominations, just as other economic things or relations such as 'commodity', 'money', 'labour-power', 'capital', means to Marx a *socio-historical fact* or something which though not physical is still given in an *empirically verifiable manner*.[34] 'As in general, with every socio-historical science, we must always keep in mind when considering the progress of economic theory, that the subject matter, here modern bourgeois society, is given in the mind of the observer just as it is in reality, and that its categories express, therefore, forms of being, modes of existence, and often only single aspects of this definite society or subject matter.'[35]

We shall later in another connection study the far-reaching theoretical and practical implications of this apparently minor difference between the scientific method of Marx and that of the classical bourgeois economists. We here confine ourselves to one most important result. The concept of *commodity*, in the specific form and context in which it appears under the conditions of the present system of 'capitalistic commodity production', includes from the very beginning a commodity of a peculiar nature, incorporating the flesh and blood in the hands and heads of the wage-labourers – the *commodity labour-power*. 'These labourers who have to sell themselves piecemeal, are a commodity like every other article of commerce, and are consequently exposed to all the vicissitudes of competition, to all the fluctuations of the market.'[36] Further, the sellers of this peculiar commodity, under the very conditions of its sale, are never in the position of free agents,[37]

---

34 See Marx's letter to Engels 2/4/58, in which he says that this concept of value 'although an abstraction, is an *historical abstraction* which, therefore, could not only be made on the basis of a particular economic development of society'. See *Selected Correspondence*, p 127.

35 See *Introduction* 1857, p 146. – See also the preceding remark on p 141 where Marx opposing his own 'theoretical' method to that hitherto applied by the classical theorists, emphasised the same point: 'Even when applying a theoretical method we must bear in mind the subject, society, as our real presupposition'.

36 See *Communist Manifesto*.

37 See the Report of the Inspectors of Factories of the six months ending April 30, 1850, p 45 – quoted by Marx in *Capital* I, p 302 footnote.

for they 'live only so long as they find work, and find work only so long as their labour increases capital.' [38]

Only by bearing in mind this specific sense in which for Marx 'commodity production' or *'general' commodity production* becomes entirely equivalent to present-day *'capitalist' commodity production* [39] can we understand the importance of that general analysis of 'commodity' which in Marx's book precedes all further analysis and critique of the capitalist mode of production. Marx is aware of the 'definite historical conditions' which are necessary in order that a product may become a 'commodity' and that, in its further development, 'money' should appear as the general commodity, for the purpose of exchange. 'The appearance of products as *commodities* pre-supposed such a development of the social division of labour, that the separation of use-value from exchange-value, a separation which first begins with barter, must already have been completed.' Again, 'the peculiar functions of *money* which it performs, either as the mere equivalent of commodities, or as means of circulation, or means of payment, as hoard or as universal money, point to very different stages in the process of social production'.[40] Yet we know by experience that a relatively primitive development of society suffices for the production of all these forms. It is otherwise with capital. 'The historical conditions of its existence are by no means given with the mere circulation of money and commodities. It can spring into life only when the owner of the means of production and subsistence meets in the market with the free labourer selling his labour-power. And this one historical condition comprises a world's history. Capital therefore, announces from its first appearance a new epoch in the process of social production.' [41]

At this stage only are we able to grasp the full importance of *industrial capital* as the only form of existence of capital which adequately represents the nature of modern capitalist production. 'Industrial capital,' according to an express assertion of Marx which we may safely take to be his final and most complete statement on this matter, 'gives to production its capitalistic character. Its existence includes that of class antagonism between capitalists and labourers. To

38   See *Communist Manifesto.*

39   See *Capital* I, p 170 footnote 1; see also *Capital* II, pp 31, 33 et seq, 116-7 etc.

40   See *Capital* I, p 170.

41   *ibid;* see also *Capital* II, p 35.

the extent that it assumes control over social production, the technique and social organisation of the labour process are revolutionised and with them the economic and historical type of society. The other kinds of capital, which appear before industrial capital amid past or declining conditions of social production, are not only subordinated to it and suffer changes in the mechanism of their functions corresponding with it, but move on it as a basis; they live and die, stand and fall, as this, their basis, lives and dies, stands and falls.' [42]

The Principle of Concrete Application

The principle of historical specification, besides its theoretical importance as an improved method of sociological analysis and research, becomes of first-rate practical importance as a polemical weapon in the disputes between the apologists defending and the critics assailing the existing conditions of society. The manner in which this weapon is wielded by the Marxists appears in the statements of Marx and Engels in replying to the bourgeois objections to communism.[43] One basic form of argument recurs in all these replies. In answer to the accusation that the Communists want to abolish property, individuality, liberty, culture, law, family, 'fatherland', etc, the Communists say that the point at issue here is not the general foundations of all social life but only the specific historical forms assumed by them in present-day bourgeois society. All economic, class and other relations which constitute the specific historical character of bourgeois society are discussed, always with the result that the would-be defenders of the natural and necessary foundations of all social order are driven to become the biased protagonists of the peculiar conditions of existing bourgeois society and the peculiar needs of the bourgeois class.

The first objection raised by the bourgeoisie to communism is that the Communists want to abolish *property*. To this the *Communist Manifesto* replies:

'The abolition of existing property relations is not all a distinctive feature of Communism.

'All property relationships in the past have been continually subject to historical change consequent upon the change in historical conditions.

42   See *Capital* 11, p 55.

43   See also the second section of the *Communist Manifesto,* 1848.

'The French Revolution, for example, abolished feudal property in favour of bourgeois property.

'The distinguishing feature of Communism is not the abolition of property generally, but the abolition of bourgeois property.

'But modern bourgeois private property is the final and most complete expression of the system of producing and appropriating products that is based on class antagonism, on the exploitation of the many by the few.

'In this sense, the theory of the Communists may be summed up in the single phrase: abolition of private property.'

It is then further argued that the property to be abolished is not the 'hard-won, personally acquired property' which, according to the ideological concept of the theoretical spokesmen of the bourgeoisie, is 'the groundwork of all personal freedom, activity and independence'. Such property really means 'the property of the petty artisan and the small peasant', a form of property that existed before the bourgeois form. The Communists have no need to abolish that. 'The development of industry has abolished it and is abolishing it daily.' 'Property in its present form moves within the antagonism of capital and wage-labour.' It has a specific and different significance for each of the two great classes confronting each other in modern bourgeois society – the bourgeoisie and the proletariat. '*To be a capitalist is to have not only a personal, but a social status in production.*' In the same way wage-labour, the labour of the proletariat, does not create individual property for the labourer: it creates capital, ie the social power that exploits wage-labour. 'The abolition of property, therefore, does not mean the transformation of personal property into social property, it is only the social character of the property that undergoes a change; it loses its class character.'

The second objection of the bourgeoisie is that the Communists want to destroy *individuality* and *freedom*. Communism replies that what is at stake here is only the 'bourgeois individuality, independence and freedom'.

'By freedom is meant, under the present bourgeois conditions of production: free trade, free selling and free buying. But if haggling disappears, free haggling disappears also. This talk about free haggling, and all other braggadocio of our bourgeoisie about freedom in general, has a meaning, if any, only in contrast with restricted haggling, with the fettered traders of the Middle Ages; but has no meaning when opposed to the Communist abolition of haggling, of the bourgeois conditions of production, and of the bourgeoisie itself.'

The bourgeois calls it an 'abolition of property' when private property is abolished. But this property, in the hands of this class, exists only by being cut off from the vast majority of society. From the moment when labour can no more be transformed into capital, money, rent; in short into a social power capable of being monopolised, the bourgeois complains that 'individuality is being destroyed'. He confesses, therefore, that by 'individuality' he means none other than that of the bourgeois, ie the capitalist owner of property. 'This individuality must, indeed, be destroyed.'

In the same way the bourgeoisie confuses the general concept of work, and *activity*, with the specific bourgeois form of wage-labour, the forced labour of the propertyless worker for the benefit of the non-labouring owners of capital. If the bourgeoisie is afraid that 'with the abolition of private property all activity will cease and universal laziness overtake us', the *Manifesto* rejoins:

'According to this, bourgeois society ought long ago to have been wrecked through sheer idleness: for those of its members who work acquire nothing and those who acquire anything do not work. The whole of this objection is but another expression of the tautology: There can no longer be any wage-labour when there is no longer any capital.'

Next, the bourgeoisie laments the threatened loss of *culture* through the advent of Communism. To this complaint also Marx has a specific reply:

'Just as to the bourgeois the disappearance of class property is the disappearance of production itself, so the disappearance of class culture is to him identical with the disappearance of all culture.

'That culture the loss of which he laments is, for the enormous majority, a mere training to act as a machine.'

As in the case of individuality, freedom and culture, the so-called menace of Communism to the *state* and the *law* is not aimed at those general functions of unifying the elements of society into a living and developing whole which have, in the past, perforce been fulfilled by state compulsion and coercive law, though in an increasingly defective manner. It is specifically directed against the present-day state which is 'only an executive committee for managing the affairs of the bourgeois class as a whole' – and against that modern bourgeois legal order which is 'only the will of the bourgeoisie made into a law for all – a will whose content is determined by the material conditions of existence of the bourgeois class'.

Abolition of the family! 'Even the most radical,' says the *Communist Manifesto*, 'flares up at this infamous purpose of the Communists.' Once more the Marxist replies specifically:

'On what foundations is the present family, the bourgeois family, based? On capital, on private gain. In its completely developed form it exists only for the bourgeoisie. But it finds its complement in the forcible absence of the family among the proletarians and in public prostitution.'

The Communists admit that they 'want to abolish the exploitation of children by their parents'.

They retort to the ever-current stupidity that 'Communists want to introduce a community of wives', that, on the contrary it is the 'present system of bourgeois marriage which is in reality a system of wives in common'.[44] For the rest, it is self-evident that 'the abolition of the present system of production must involve the abolition of the community of women arising out of that system, that is, of prostitution both official and unofficial'.

To the further charge made by the nationalists that Communism is going to 'abolish the Fatherland' the *Manifesto* replies that in present-day bourgeois society 'the workers have no Fatherland'. 'One cannot take from them what they do not have.'[45] On the contrary, as Engels pointed out; the ancient communal property in land has been, for all free men, 'a real Fatherland, ie an inherited free communal property'.[46]

The attitude of the proletariat of each country with regard to the so-called national interests depends upon the specific stage reached by the workers' movement in its development on a national and international scale:

44   This statement calls to mind the remark of a Turkish ambassador made to Voltaire that 'you Christians keep your seraglios without any further expense in the house of your friends' (reported by Hume in Essays XIX). A similar statement is made by the De Goncourts as to the system of marriage prevailing among the bourgeoisie at their time.

45   The conclusion that the general notions of Fatherland, Religion, Morals, Loyalty to the Government etc lose all meaning for the vast majority of the people, because 'without property, they have no Fatherland, without Fatherland, everybody is against them, and they themselves must be up in arms against everybody', had already been brought forward by the bourgeois revolutionist *Brissot* in his *Observations d'un républicain sur les différents systèmes d'amministration provinciales*, 1787 (See Marx's excerpts in MEGA I, 6, pp 616-17).

46   See Engels' article on 'The Mark' (appendix to first German edition of *Socialism, Utopian and Scientific*, 1882).

'In so far as the exploitation of one individual by another is abolished, the exploitation of one nation by another is also abolished. With the disappearance of the antagonism between classes within the nation, the hostility of one nation to another will disappear.'

Again, in reply to 'the indictments levelled against Communism from a religious, philosophical, and generally, from an ideological standpoint', the *Manifesto* summarily points to the specific historical character of all human ideas:

'What else does the history of ideas prove than that intellectual production changes its character as material production is changed? The ruling ideas of an age have ever been only the ideas of the ruling class.

'When the ancient world was in decline, the ancient religions were conquered by Christianity. When Christian ideas succumbed in the eighteenth century to the ideas of Enlightenment, feudal society fought its death battle with the then revolutionary bourgeoisie. The ideas of religious liberty and freedom of conscience merely expressed the sway of free competition within the domain of knowledge.'

To that fraction of the bourgeoisie which concedes that religious, moral, philosophical, political, legal ideas, etc, have been modified in the course of historical development, but at the same time reproaches Communism for abolishing the *eternal truths* common to all social conditions, such as freedom, justice, etc, for doing away with religion and morality altogether, instead of remoulding them – Marx replies that *even in this most general form, traditional ideas still retain a specific historical element.* They do not depend any longer on the definite form which class antagonisms have assumed in a given epoch of social development. They do depend, however, on the historical fact continuing through all these epochs – the existence of class antagonisms:

'Whatever form they may have taken, one fact is common to all past ages, viz the exploitation of one part of society by the other. No wonder, then, that the social consciousness of all past ages, despite the multiplicity and variety it displays, moves within certain common forms, or general ideas, which cannot completely vanish except with the total disappearance of class antagonism.

'The Communist revolution is the most radical rupture with traditional property relations, no wonder, then, that its development involves the most radical rupture with traditional ideas.'

Principle of Revolutionary Change

Traditional theory of society, spread over several hundred years and split into many schools and currents, does not present itself to the present-day observer as a homogeneous entity. This is true even if we disregard the fundamental divergence which has appeared within bourgeois thought since the beginning of the nineteenth century, when a new and predominantly *historical* current opposed itself – at first with a monopolistic claim, later only as a supplementary second form – to the hitherto prevailing *theoretical* approach.

The classical phase of bourgeois social theory, continuing into the first decades of the nineteenth century, is characterised by an unsophisticated generalisation of the new bourgeois principles. Later, in the hands of the 'vulgar' economists of the nineteenth century, this unsophisticated attitude became a more or less conscious tendency to represent the economic system of bourgeois society in contrast to its politics – or at least bourgeois production as distinguished from distribution – as a general and unchangeable form of all social life. Finally, the founders of modern 'economics', and the corresponding schools of 'general' or 'formal' sociology, have even emphasised the 'unspecific' treatment of their subject matter as the very criterion of their new and assumedly 'disinterested' scientism. A more detailed analysis will be necessary to point out in each of these currents a modern bourgeois social theory the special manner in which the *a priori* of definite premises evolving out of the historical and class-conditioned position of all bourgeois science, penetrates into the methods and results of the investigator and into the concepts and propositions set up by the theorist.

A further complication is added by the fact that, in dealing with contemporary bourgeois social theory, we can often no longer exactly determine how far it already represents a reaction to the attack of the proletarian class. The origin of not a few among the most important of its later developments is to be directly traced to the Marxist theory. We mention particularly, from the last two generations of German sociologists, jurists, historians, and philosophers, Tönnies and Stammler, Max Weber and Troeltsch, Scheler and Mannheim; and among the economists, as not the most important but perhaps the most typical representative of this whole group – Werner Sombart. The manifold broken and distorted forms assumed by the controversy with Marxism, under the special conditions of German academic science, appear most strikingly in the last named German savant. Werner Sombart originally was – or at least believed himself to be – a thorough-going Marxist, but later, with the changing political and social conditions leading up to the present regime of a so-called 'National Socialism' in Germany, changed heart and finally became an outright anti-Marxist.[47] Notwithstanding these distortions, the irresistible influence exercised by Marx's theory on all present-day bourgeois social science is clearly evident even in the later career of Sombart. As late as 1927, in the introduction to the third volume of his main economic work, he testified to the fact that 'all that is good in this work is due to Marx'.[48] One year later, at the Zürich Sociological Conference, he volunteered a 'personal confession' that he had been a 'convinced Marxist' up to 1894. On the same occasion he claimed to have been the first to enunciate the principle of the so-called 'non-evaluative character of a genuine sociological science', and traced back the origin of this well-known doctrine of contemporary social research to the 'contradiction' which had at that early time arisen within himself, ie between his internal Marxist 'conviction', and his worldly position as a 'Royal Prussian University Professor'.[49]

For all these reasons, in confronting the general principles of the Marxist theory with bourgeois science we shall not so much refer to the more recent displays of contemporary social thought in which their persisting difference is already modified to a certain extent by mutual interaction. We shall rather try to bring out the underlying fundamental contrast in that pure form in which it originally appeared in the classical and post-classical bourgeois writers of the eighteenth and early nineteenth centuries on the one hand, and in the writings of Marx and Engels on the other.

47   We mention from the writings of Sombart, in which this development is reflected, the following:
     1894 et seq. Review articles and books, Marxist in tendency; among them the first scientific appreciation of the third volume of Capital in Archiv für soziale Bewegung, VII.
     1897. First edition of the book Socialism and Social Movements in the 19th Century. 1900, pamphlet, Nevertheless! Theoretical and Historical Notes on the Labour Trade Union Movement.
     1924. Tenth and 'fully revised' edition of the book Socialism and Social Movements under the changed title Proletarian Socialism (Marxism).
     Subsequent to Hitler's accession to power a new book German Socialism, etc.
     Compare also the articles on Sombart's career by Rosa Luxemburg in Neue Zeit XVIII, 2, pp 740 et seq ('The "German science" behind the workers'), and by the present writer in Archiv für die Geschichte des Sozialismus und der Arbeiterbewegung XVI.

48   See Sombart, Modern Capitalism, volume III (1927) p XIX ('und alles, was etwas Gutes in meinem Werke ist, verdankt es dem Geiste Marx').

49   See the record of the Proceedings of the Conference.

Classical bourgeois economists concern themselves with existing bourgeois society. They ingenuously regard society's basic relationships as having the immutable character of a genuine natural law, and are for just this reason unable to become aware of or to investigate scientifically any other than this actually given form of society.

Even when bourgeois social theorists appear to speak of other social forms, their real subject matter is still the prevailing form of bourgeois society whose main characteristics they find duplicated in all other forms. When they speak of 'society' in general, we can still recognise, with only slight variations, in this figure of so-called general society the well-known features of present-day bourgeois society. This is most evident in the writings of the great founders of bourgeois social science in the seventeenth and eighteenth centuries and their followers, the German idealistic philosophers from Kant to Hegel, who naïvely used not only the term 'society', but even the term 'civil society', as a timeless concept.[50]

Even when bourgeois investigators speak of a historical 'development' of society, they do not step beyond the magic circle of bourgeois society. They consider all the earlier forms as 'preliminary stages' leading up to the present more or less fully developed form of society. They constantly apply the concepts drawn from actual social conditions to the preceding historical forms. Right into the nineteenth century they describe those phases of primitive history which can not possibly be represented by the categories of modern bourgeois society, ie property, state, family, etc, as not belonging to history proper, but as merely 'prehistoric'. Even Johann Gottfried Herder, who stood in a much closer relation to real history than most of his contemporaries, wrote i his Diary: 'How many ages may have passed by before we learned know or think? The Phoenician? The Ethiopian? Or none of these Are we then, with our Moses, in the right place?'[51]

Just as in their study of past conditions, so in their analysis c present tendencies, bourgeois social theorists remain tied to the bourg eois categories. They simply cannot conceive of any future change other than those resulting from an 'evolutionary' development, an which reveal no breach with the fundamental principles of the presen day bourgeois order of society. They regard all social revolutions a

---

50   See Marx, German Ideology.

51—See J. G. Herder, Journal meiner Reise 1769.

pathological interferences with 'normal' social development.[52] They expect, after the revolutionary 'cycle' has run its full course, pre-revolutionary *social conditions* to be re-established as unchanged in their fundamentals, as according to a similar theory (held by the politicians) *political conditions* of the ancien régime are finally re-established by the 'Restoration'. They hold all tendencies of revolutionary socialism and communism which aim at any thing beyond this, as mere 'disturbance of healthy social progress' and, theoretically, as 'unscientific' fantasies.

Marx's social science is fundamentally opposed to all these traditional concepts of classical bourgeois theory. This contrast is, however, not so simple that it can be reduced to the biblical formula 'Let your speech be yea, yea – nay, nay'. It would be altogether wrong, for instance, to imagine that since the bourgeois theory is the doctrine of a 'bourgeois society', Marx's socialist theory must necessarily be the doctrine of a 'socialist society'. As a matter of fact, scientific socialism is not at all concerned with the painting of a future state of society. Marx leaves that to the sectarians of the old and new Utopias. He, according to his materialistic principle, deals with the real form of society which exists today, ie bourgeois society. Thus Marx, as against the bourgeois 'theorists' who continually tend to generalise in one way or another the facts they 'discover', more nearly approaches the method of the classical bourgeois historians, from which however, in another direction, he kept himself all the more aloof through his insistence upon a strictly theoretical form of scientific knowledge.

Nor is the bourgeois concept of developmental stages wholly repudiated by Marx. He plainly distinguishes the historical forms of 'Asiatic', 'Antique' and 'Feudal' society, and groups them, together with modern 'Bourgeois' society, into a series of *'progressive epochs of socio-economic formation'*. Although he does no more regard, as the bourgeois theorists had done, all previous forms of society as mere preliminary steps to its present and final formation, still he indulges in the statement that the present form of society is itself merely the last of a series of preliminary steps and, as it were, 'concludes the pre-history of a really human society'.[53] He does not raise a fundamental objection

52 Thus Comte regarded revolutionary periods of society as analogous to disease in the human body. He did not, for this reason, ignore them totally but rather, following the physician Broussais (who first subjected the phenomena of disease to the laws governing healthy bodies) proclaimed the study of this *'pathologie sociale'* as a possible substitute for the experimental method used by the physicists.

53 See *Preface*, 1859.

to the extension of scientific concepts derived from the present bourgeois state of society to the conditions of past historical epochs. He explicitly states the principle that the categories of bourgeois society as
the 'most developed and most complex historical organisation of production', furnish a key to the understanding of earlier epochs of social
and economic formation.[54] He even endorsed, in his early years, the
'correct idea' underlying that 'common fiction of the eighteenth century, which regarded the primitive state of man as the true state of
human nature'.[55] It is true that he later replaced this revolutionary
slogan of the eighteenth century, and the fresh impetus which it had in
the meantime received through the first great discoverers of primitive
society in the nineteenth century, by the more sober principles of a
strictly empirical and materialistic research. However, he did not even
then abandon the underlying idea but rather reshaped it in a critical
spirit and gave it a new and fruitful application. In the same way even
the bourgeois idea of 'evolution' was not completely wiped out in
Marx's theory of a social revolution. Just as there is – in spite of all the
intervening revolutions, and in fact, realised just by these revolutions –
one progressive line of development leading up from the historic and
'pre-historic' past to the contemporary form of bourgeois society, so
will the future socialist and communist society, springing from the
social revolution, though involving a fundamental transformation of
the present-day bourgeois order, still remain, according to Marx, an
outgrowth of existing conditions of society.

Principle of Revolutionary Practice (Praxis)

The Marxist critique of the developmental concept of bourgeois social
science starts from a recognition of the illusionary character of that
'so-called historical evolution', according to which 'the last stage regards the preceding stages as being only preliminary to itself, and
therefore can only look at them onesidedly'.[56] Just where Marx seems
to adopt this naïve pseudo-Darwinian metaphysics of evolution, which

54   See Introduction 1857, p 145.

55   See 'The Philosophical Manifesto of the Historical School of Law', in
Rheinische Zeitung, 1842, No 221, Supplement (MEGA I, 1, p 251): 'The
correct idea underlying all these eccentricities (of the Historical School) is that
those primitive conditions are naïve, "Dutch pictures" of the real conditions.'
In Lloyd Easton and Kurt Guddat (eds), Writings of the Young Marx on
Philosophy and Society, New York 1967, pp 96-105.

56   See Introduction, 1857, p 145.

later was fully and blindly accepted by such orthodox Marxists as Kautsky,[57] and on account of which such heterodox Marxists as Georges Sorel have altogether denied any application of the principle of evolution to scientific sociology,[58] he actually reverses the whole conception and thereby destroys its metaphysical character. While bourgeois evolutionists imagine, with Spencer, that they can explain the more complex organisation of the higher types both of animal species and social forms by reference to the simpler organisation of the lower, Marx breaks up this illusion with the paradoxical statement that *'the anatomy of man is a key to the anatomy of the ape'*.[59]

This critical consciousness breaks the magic spell of the metaphysical 'law' of evolution. From a valid *a priori* axiom, it is reduced to a working hypothesis which must be empirically verified in each case. Even though bourgeois society does provide a 'key' to ancient society, it does not therefore follow that such categories as commodity, money, state, law, etc, must have the same meaning for ancient society and its mode of production as they have for modern capitalist production and for the bourgeois society which is based upon it. Thus, the path is made free for a strictly empirical research. Bourgeois society may contain the relations of earlier societies in a further developed form. It may contain them as well in degenerate, stunted and travestied forms (as, eg the communal property of primitive times, according to Marx, was contained in a travestied form in the Russia 'Mir').[60] It likewise contains within itself the germs of future developments of present society, though by no means their complete determination. The false idealistic concept of evolution as applied by bourgeois social theorists, is *closed* on both sides, and in all past and future forms of society rediscovers only itself. The new, critical and materialistic Marxist principle of development is, on the other hand, *open* on both sides. Marx does not deal with Asiatic, Antique, or Feudal society, and still less with those primitive societies which preceded all written history, merely as 'preliminary stages' of contemporary society. He regards them, in their totality, as so many independent historical formations which are

57 See the author's *The Materialistic Conception of History (A Critical Examination of the Work of Karl Kautsky)* Leipzig 1929, pp 32 et seq. (Only available in German.)

58 See *Introduction à l'èconomie moderne*, 1903; also *Illusions du progrés*, 3rd ed, pp 239-44.

59 See *Introduction*, 1857, p 145.

60 *ibid.*

to be understood in terms of their own categories. In the same way he defines the socialist and communist society arising out of the proletarian revolution not only as a further developed form of bourgeois society, but as a new type which is no longer to be basically explained by any of the bourgeois categories. Marx's quarrel with the *Utopian socialists* is not, as many have imagined, inspired by their idea of a future state, totally different from that of contemporary bourgeois society, leaving out the shadows. All such utopian schemes will, when worked out in detail and put into practice, inevitably reproduce only the same old bourgeois form of society we know so well.[61] On the other hand, Marxism, while carefully avoiding a detailed painting of future stages of development, nevertheless endeavours, in its materialistic analysis and critique of the specific historical features of contemporary bourgeois society, to find the main tendencies of the further development leading up, first to that transitional stage which is opened by the proletarian revolution, and ultimately, to that further advanced stage which Marx calls the *completely developed communistic society*. Communistic society in its 'first phase', as it is just emerging from the womb of bourgeois society after long labour pains, is still in many ways, in its economic, political, legal, intellectual and moral structure, determined by bourgeois principles. Communistic society in its 'second phase', where it has already developed on its own basis, will be as far remote from the principles of present-day bourgeois society, as, in the other direction, the classless and stateless 'primitive communism' of the earliest epochs of human society is removed from contemporary society. Communistic society, when it is fully developed, will have left the narrow bourgeois horizon far behind and will ultimately realise the slogan which, in an abstract form, was first enunciated by the 'utopian' pioneers on the threshold of the nineteenth century: 'From each according to his abilities, to each according to his needs.'[62]

To the philosophical dialectic of Hegel, which he otherwise regarded as the perfected instrument of a *developmental investigation of society*, Marx raised the objection that, in the 'mystified form' in which it became fashionable in Germany, it 'seemed to glorify existing conditions'. On the other hand, the new and rational form in which this Hegelian dialectic reappears in Marxist social research, has became 'a

61   See Marx, *Class struggles in France*, Section III (first appeared in *Neue Rheinische Zeitung, Politisch-ökonomische Revue*, Hamburg 1850).

62   See Marx, 'Marginal Notes to the Program of the German Labor Party 1875' (*Neue Zeit* IX, 1, p 567), in *Selected Works*, pp 315-335.

scandal and abomination to the bourgeoisie and its doctrinaire spokes-men; because it includes in its positive understanding of existing con-ditions at the same time an understanding of their negation and of their necessary disintegration; because it conceives of every form manifested as being in the flux of movement, ie also from its transitory aspect; because it lets nothing impose upon it, and because it is essentially critical and revolutionary'.[63] The outstanding difference between Marx and Hegel in this respect, is evident without a more detailed analysis. Hegel, who glorified existing institutions and moderate progress within the narrow confines of the contemporary Prussian State,[64] explicitly limited the validity of his dialectical principle to the *past* development of society and consigned future progress in a purposely irrational manner to the 'mole, burrowing below the surface'.[65] Again, though criticising the so-called 'Pre-formation Hypothesis', according to which all future forms are already physically contained in those that precede them, he emphasised at the same time the correctness of the idea underlying this hypothesis, ie the assumption that social development 'remains by itself in its process and that by such a development no new content is brought about, but only a change of form'. Development is, therefore, according to Hegel, 'only to be regarded as if it were a play; the something else which is set by it, is in fact nothing else'.[66] It is evident that from this standpoint which, in its unyielding Hegelian formula, amounts almost to an involuntary criticism of the principle of evolution as used by the bourgeois social investigators, there is no room for the *conscious human-social act*, which will radically trans-form and overthrow the present order of society. Hegel said, concern-ing the real 'purpose' of all historical action, that 'it is already fulfilled in truth, and need not wait for us'. Its actual performance, then, only 'removes the semblance as if it were not yet performed'.[67] Hence, in contrast to some of his followers, who later on actually tried to use his dialectical method as an instrument for revolution, Hegel considered the only purpose of his philosophy to be to 're-establish' the conviction

---

63   See Marx, *Postscript*, 1873.

64   See Hegel's address to his audience on the occasion of his opening lecture in Berlin on October 22, 1818.

65   See the peroration of Hegel's lectures on the History of Philosophy (1817-1830).

66   See Hegel, *Encyclopaedia* I §161 (1818-1827).

67   *ibid*, addition to §212.

from which 'every unsophisticated consciousness proceeds': *'What is reasonable is real, and what is real is reasonable'*, and thus to bring about the final *'reconciliation'* between 'reason as self-conscious mind' and 'reason as a given reality'.[68]

It is here that we face the most important consequence of the total destruction of bourgeois evolutionary metaphysics which is implied in Marx's materialistic criticism of the Hegelian idealist dialectic. Marx's study of society is based upon a full recognition of the *reality of historical change*. Marx treats all conditions of existing bourgeois society as changing, ie more exactly, as conditions in the process of being changed by human actions. Bourgeois society is not, according to Marx, a general entity which can be replaced by another stage in a historical movement. It is both the result of an earlier phase and the starting point of a new phase, of the social class war which is leading to a social revolution.

68   See Hegel, *Preface to Philosophy of Law* (1820).

Introduction to *Capital*

Marx's book on capital, like Plato's book on the state, like Machia-
velli's *Prince* and Rousseau's *Social Contract*, owes its tremendous and
enduring impact to the fact that it grasps and articulates, at a tu ning
point of history, the full implications of the new force breaking in
upon the old forms of life. All the economic, political, and social
questions, upon which the analysis in Marx's *Capital* theoretically
devolves, are today world-shaking practical issues, over which the real-
life struggle between great social forces, between states and classes,
rages in every corner of the earth. Karl Marx proved himself to pos-
terity to be the great forward-looking thinker of his age, in as much
as he comprehended early on how decisive these questions would be
for the approaching world-historical crisis. But even as great a thinker
as Marx could not have grasped these questions theoretically and incorporated them in his work, had they not already been posed, in
some form or another, as actual problems in the real life of his own
epoch.

* Originally published as the introduction to Korsch's edition of *Das
Kapital* in Berlin 1932. Translated by T. M. Holmes from the text as reprinted
in the Ullstein paperback edition of Volume I, 1970.

Fate treated this German veteran of '48 in a peculiar way. He was banished, by both republican and absolutist governments, from the original context of his practical activity, and thus removed in good time from the narrow, backward conditions of Germany, and projected into the historical mainstream which was to be the setting for his real achievements. By the age of 30 Karl Marx had achieved, through his study of Hegel's thought, a profound and comprehensive, albeit *philosophical,* grasp of life. But now, precisely in consequence of the forcible transposition of his fields of operations, before and after the failed revolution of 1848, he was able, during his successive periods of exile, firstly in Belgium and France, and later in England, to come into immediate theoretical and practical contact with the most progressive developments in the real life of that time.

On the one hand there were the *French socialist and communist movements,* advancing beyond the achievements of the great jacobin-bourgeois revolution towards new, proletarian objectives; and on the other hand the *fully developed structure of modern capitalist production, with its corresponding relations of production and distribution,* which had emerged in England from the Industrial Revolution of 1770-1830. These elements of Marx's vision – French political history, English economic development, the modern labour movement – all 'transcended' the contemporary scene in Germany, and Marx devoted decades of thought and research to the incorporation of these elements into his scientific work – especially into his magnum opus, *Capital.* It was this combination of sustained energy and wide-ranging vision that lent to *Capital* the extraordinary vitality by virtue of which it remains entirely 'topical' in the present day. One might even say that in many respects it is only now beginning to come into its own.

'The ultimate objective of this work' is, in the words of the author, 'to reveal the economic laws of motion of modern society.' This statement already implies that *Capital* is not meant to be simply a contribution to the traditional academic study of economics. It is true, of course, that the book did play an important part in the development of economic theory, and has left its imprint on the technical literature of the subject right up to the present day. But *Capital* is also, as its sub-title declares, a 'Critique of Political Economy',[1]

1   The sub-title, that is, of the second German edition, to which Korsch refers throughout. In this translation, however, quotations and chapter-numeration has been brought into line with the most accessible English editions (Moscow, and Lawrence and Wishart). These are based on the 1887 Moore-Aveling translation, itself based on the third German edition which was published after Marx's death.

and this rubric signifies much more than the adoption of a critical attitude towards the individual doctrines advanced by this or that economic theorist; in Marx's terms it signifies a critique of political economy *as such*. Looked at from the standpoint of Marx's historical-materialist approach, political economy is, after all, not just a theoretical system involving true or false propositions. It embodies in itself an aspect of historical reality – or, to be more precise, it is one aspect of the 'modern bourgeois mode of production' and of the social formation that is built on it, one aspect, that is, of the particular historical reality which is critically analysed in *Capital* from its inception through its development and demise to its eventual transition to new and higher forms of production and society. If we think in terms of the academic categories we are used to today, then Marx's *Capital* appears to be more an historical and sociological, rather than an economic theory.

But even this revised definition of Marx's work, and the series of similar qualifications we might add, do not succeed in characterising the full range and depth of the Marxian scientific method and its subject matter. *Capital* does not belong to any one discipline, but neither is it a kind of philosophical allsorts, for it deals with a quite definite object from a quite particular standpoint. In this respect Marx's work may be compared with the famous book by Darwin on the *Origin of Species*. Just as Darwin discovered the laws of development of organic nature, so Marx revealed the laws governing the course of human history. Marx approached these laws in two ways: on the one hand he outlined the general historical law of development, which is called 'historical materialism', and on the other he propounded the particular law of motion of the modern capitalist mode of production and the bourgeois society it gives rise to. The comparison of Marx with Darwin is not based simply on the pure coincidence of historical dates (though it is true that the *Origin of Species* and the first part of Marx's work on capitalism, *A Contribution to the Critique of Political Economy*, both appeared in 1859). As Marx himself suggested, and as Engels made clear in his speech at Marx's graveside, the comparison expresses a much deeper connection than this. In one of those profound and exquisite, though often seemingly digressive footnotes with which Marx almost overloads *Capital*, he relates how Darwin first drew his attention to the 'history of natural technology' that is, to the 'formation of plant and animal organisms as instruments for the sustenance of plant and animal life'. And he poses the question

'Does not the history of the productive organs of social man, of organs that are the material basis of all social organisation, deserve equal attention? And would not such a history be easier to compile, since, as Vico says, human history differs from natural history in this, that we have made the former but not the latter?'

These remarks express perfectly the relation between Darwin and Marx, stressing not only what they have in common, but also the distinction between them. Darwin's study deals with natural history in the narrower sense, whereas Marx deals with a practical socio-historical development, which man not only experiences, but also shapes. Marx, however, unlike some of the modern obscurantists and demi-theologians of the so-called 'humanities', did not draw the conclusion that the description and study of man's social life permits a lesser degree of intellectual and empirical rigour and a higher ratio of subjectivity than the natural sciences themselves. Marx was inclined to work from the opposite position, and explicitly set himself the task of outlining the economic development of society as a 'natural-historical' process.

We are not yet in a position to judge whether, or to what extent, Marx carried out this imposing project in *Capital*. That could only be decided in some future age, when, as Marx anticipated, his theory would no longer be subjected to the 'prejudices of so-called public opinion', but would be assessed on the basis of a truly 'scientific criticism'. As things stand at present, however, this is still a long-term prospect.

While it might be impertinent to attempt such a definitive judgement at the present time, it is appropriate to provide this edition of Marx's *Capital* with an indication at least of the rather peculiar relationship between the realised and the unrealised portions of the work.

Marx's work on economics presents itself to us today as a gigantic torso – and this aspect is not likely to be substantially altered by the appearance of the hitherto unpublished material still extant. Let us leave out of account for now the very broad outlines of Marx's earlier drafts, in which the critique of political economy is not yet isolated from the critique of law and government, from ideological forms in general, is not yet distinguished as an autonomous and primary object of investigation – even then there remains an enormous gap between what Marx planned and what he actually carried out in his work.

In 1850 Marx settled in London where 'The enormous material on the history of political economy which is accumulated in the British Museum; the favourable view which London offers for the observation of bourgeois society; finally the new stage of development which the latter seemed to have entered with the discovery of gold in California and Australia' decided him to begin his political-economic studies again 'from the very beginning'. In the period after his arrival in London Marx commented twice on the overall plan of the political-economic work he had in mind, firstly in the manuscript of the 'General Introduction', written down in 1857, but subsequently 'suppressed' until Kautsky published it in the *Neue Zeit* in 1903; and secondly in the 'Preface' to the *Critique of Political Economy*, which made its appearance in 1859. Here is the first of these two comments: 'The order of treatment must manifestly be as follows: first, the general abstract definitions which are more or less applicable to all forms of society. . . . Second, the categories which go to make up the inner organisation of bourgeois society and constitute the foundations of the principal classes; capital, wage-labour, landed property; their mutual relations; city and country; the three great social classes, the exchange between them; circulation, credit (private). Third, the organisation of bourgeois society in the form of a state, considered in relation to itself; the "unproductive" classes; taxes; public debts; public credit; population; colonies; emigration. Fourth, the international organisation of production; international division of labour; international exchange; import and export; rate of exchange. Fifth, the world market and crises.'

Two years later Marx published 'the first two chapters of the first section of the first book on capital' as a separate 'Part I' (some 200 pages long!) entitled *A Contribution to the Critique of Political Economy*. He began the *Preface* to this work with these words: 'I consider the system of bourgeois economy in the following order: capital, landed property, wage-labour; state, foreign trade, world market. Under the first three heads I examine the conditions of the existence of the three great classes which make up modern bourgeois society; the connection of the three remaining heads is self-evident.'

Only a fragment of the first half of these comprehensive plans is realised in the work on capital that was actually completed, partly by Marx himself, and partly by others. At the end of 1862, when he had already decided that the 'continuation' of the *Critique of Political Economy* should be published by itself under the title *Capital*, he wrote to Kugelmann that this new book (by which he meant not only Volume I of *Capital* as we know it today, but all the other parts too!) 'really only deals with those matters which should form the third chapter of the first section, namely capital in general'. For a variety of reasons, some internal to the work and others extraneous, Marx decided at about this time to cut down appreciably on the overall plan which he had maintained virtually unaltered up until then. He decided that he would present the whole of the material in three or four books, the first of which would deal with the 'Productive Process of Capital', the second with the 'Process of Circulation', the third with the 'Structure of the Overall Process' and the fourth with the 'History of the Theory'.

Marx himself only completed one of these four books of *Capital*. It appeared as Volume I of *Capital* in 1867 and a second edition followed in 1872. After Marx's death his friend and literary collaborator Friedrich Engels pieced together the second and third books on the basis of the available manuscripts. They were published as Volumes II and III of *Capital* in 1885 and 1894. There are also the three volumes entitled *Theories of Surplus Value,* which were published by Kautsky between 1905 and 1910, again on the basis of Marx's manuscripts, and which may be thought in a sense to stand for the fourth book of *Capital*. Strictly speaking, however, they are not a continuation of *Capital*, but an incomplete version of an older manuscript which Marx wrote as early as August 1861-June 1863. This was not intended to be a part of *Capital* but forms the continuation of the *Critique of Political Economy* of 1859. Engels himself planned to publish the critical part of this manuscript as Volume IV of *Capital* after excising the numerous passages he had already used to build out Volumes II and III. But what Marx does in Volume I runs counter to this intention. Not even that part of the manuscript that had already been published in *A Contribution to the Critique of Poliitcal Economy* is taken over unaltered, but is rather submitted to a thorough revision in the first three chapters of the new work. One of the most important tasks of future editors of Marx will be to provide a complete and unabridged version of the manuscript of the *Contribution to a Critique of Political Economy*; for this is the earliest general exposition of Marx's system of thought, and indeed the only one that he ever completed himself.

Although there is an enormous gap between the project that was contemplated and the work that was completed, Marx's *Capital* —

even the first volume on its own – impresses us both in form and content, as a finished and rounded whole. We should not imagine that while Marx was at work on Volume I he saw the other volumes completed in his mind's eye, and deployed in the first book a strictly apportioned one-quarter of all his thoughts on the subject. This conception is discredited by something that Rosa Luxemburg emphasised 30 years ago in an excellent study of *Capital*. She wrote that decades before the appearance at last of the third volume in 1894, 'Marx's doctrine as a whole had been popularised and accepted' in Germany and in other countries 'on the basis of the first volume', which revealed 'not a trace of theoretical incompleteness'.

There is little sense in trying to solve this apparent contradiction between the content and the reception of *Capital* by saying that this first volume already gives a complete picture of the relation between the two great classes in modern bourgeois society, the capitalist class and the working class, as well as describing the overall tendency of present-day capitalist development towards socialisation of the means of production, while the questions that are dealt with in the subsequent volumes, the circulation of capital and the distribution of the whole surplus value between the different forms of capitalists' income (such as profit, interest, ground-rent, and trading profit), are of less theoretical and practical relevance for the working class. Quite apart from the fact that Marx's theory in *Capital* states that there are three and not two basic classes in bourgeois society (capitalists, wage-labourers and landowners), it would be an unthinkable over-simplification of the theory to say that it derives the laws of motion and development of modern society solely from the sphere of production and the conflicts and contradictions arising in this sphere, and that it does not take account in this connection of the process of circulation too, and of the structural integration of both aspects in the overall process.

The real answer to the problem is that the investigation Marx undertakes in the first volume is only *formally* limited to the productive process of capitalism. In actual fact, in his treatment of this *aspect*, Marx grasps and portrays the *totality* of the capitalist mode of production, and the bourgeois society that emerges from it. He describes and connects all its economic features, together with its legal, political, religious, artistic, and philosophical – in short, *ideological* – manifestations. This comprehensiveness is a necessary consequence of the *dialectical mode of description*, an Hegelian legacy which Marx appropriates formally intact, despite his materialistic 'reversal' of its philosophical-idealist content. The dialectic may be compared with the modern axiomatic method of the mathematical sciences, in so far as this method uses an apparently logical-constructive procedure to deduce from certain simple principles the results already arrived at through detailed research.

This is not the place to weigh up the advantages and disadvantages of applying the dialectical method to political economy. Suffice it to say that this method is used, with consummate skill, in *Capital*, and that its employment for an examination of the process of production implies the necessity of including in this investigation the whole of the capitalist mode of production and the bourgeois society based upon it. Now there are a number of difficulties which arise for the uninitiated reader precisely out of the peculiar 'simplicity' of the conceptual development of the first few chapters of *Capital*. These difficulties are bound up with the dialectical mode of description, and I shall deal with them later on.

This, then, is the most important reason why the first volume of *Capital* shows 'no trace of theoretical incompleteness', why this, the only part of the work finished off by Marx himself, gives, despite the author's explicit and oft-reiterated limitation of its formal purview to the 'productive process of capitalism', a much greater impression of unity than does the complete work formed by the addition of the subsequent volumes. But there is another reason too, and that is the *artistic* form which Volume I achieves as a whole, in spite of a style that often seems stiff and unnecessarily constrained. Marx once wrote a placatory letter to Engels in response to his friend's good-humoured complaints about the protracted delay in producing this work; the words of this letter are applicable not only to *Capital*, but also to some of Marx's historical works, especially *The Eighteenth Brumaire of Louis Bonaparte*:

'Whatever shortcomings they may have, the merit of my writings is that they are an artistic whole, and that can only be attained by my method of never having them printed until they lie before me as a *whole*. This is impossible with the Jacob Grimm method, which is in general more suited to works not dialectically constructed.' (Marx: Letter to Engels, 31st July, 1865)

Capital presents itself to us then, as an 'artistic whole' or a 'scientific work of art': it has a strong and compelling attraction for any reader who comes to it free from prejudice, and this æsthetic attraction will help the beginner to overcome both the alleged and the genuine difficulties of the book. Now there is something rather peculiar about these difficulties. With one qualification, which will be elaborated in due course, we can safely say that *Capital* contains, for the kind of audience Marx had in mind ('I assume of course they will be readers who want to learn something new, who will be prepared to think while they are reading'), fewer difficulties than any of the more-or-less widely read manuals on economics. The reader who is at all capable of thinking for himself is hardly likely to meet serious difficulties, even with terminology. Some sections, such as chapters 10 and 13-15, on 'The Working Day', 'Co-operation', 'Division of Labour', and 'Machinery and Modern Industry', and Part VIII on 'Primitive Accumulation', all of which Marx assured Kugelmann would be 'immediately comprehensible' to his wife, are indeed so predominantly descriptive and narrative – and the description is so vivid, the narration so gripping – that they can be immediately understood by anyone; and these chapters together constitute more than two-fifths of the whole book.

There are a number of other chapters, however, which do not belong to this descriptive type, and yet are virtually as easy to read, besides having the additional merit that they lead us directly to the heart of *Capital*. That is why I want to recommend to the beginner an approach that diverges somewhat from Marx's advice on a suitable start for the ladies (wherein we may sense a certain deference to the prejudices of his own time!). I hope that the approach I recommend will enable the reader to attain a full understanding of *Capital* just as readily, or even more readily than if he were to begin with the difficult opening chapters.

It is best, I think, to begin with a thorough perusal of Chapter 7 on 'The Labour Process and the Process of Producing Surplus-Value'. There are, it is true, a number of preliminary difficulties to be overcome, but these are all internal to the matter in hand, and not due, as are many difficulties in the preceding chapters, to a really rather unnecessary artificiality in the presentation. What is said here refers directly and immediately to palpable realities, and in the first instance to the palpable reality of the human *work process*. We encounter straightaway a clear and stark presentation of an insight essential for the proper understanding of *Capital* – the insight that this real-life work process represents, under the present régime of the *capitalist mode of production*, not only the production of use-values for human needs, but also the production of saleable goods – commercial values, exchange-values, or to put it simply, 'values'. In this chapter the reader becomes acquainted, in the context of actual production, with the dual nature of the capitalist *mode of production*, and with the split character of *labour* itself, in so far as labour is carried out by wage-labourers for the owners of the means of production, in so far, that is, as proletarians work for capitalists. Given these insights the reader will be in a better position later on to understand the far more difficult investigation in the first three chapters, of the dual character of *commodity-producing labour* and the antithesis of *commodity* and *money*.

But we are not really in a position to tackle this just yet. For the time being we shall leave aside altogether those first chapters which have proved such a stumbling-block for generations of Marx readers, even though a considerable amount of their content would be accessible to us after having studied Chapter 7, especially the analysis of the 'Substance of Value and the Magnitude of Value' in the first two sections of the first chapter. Marx declared, in the Preface to the first German edition that he had 'popularised' his treatment of these matters 'as much as possible' compared with their presentation in the *Critique of Political Economy*. But the third section on the 'Form of Value' is nowhere near as easy; in the thirteen years between 1859 and 1872 Marx revised this section no less than four times, and it does 'indeed deal with subtleties'. Nor is the fourth section, on the 'Fetishism of Commodities' very easy to read, but this is for different reasons, which will be gone into presently. The brief second chapter is quite easy, but the third is again extremely hard for the novice.

It is better then for the complete beginner not to try to come to grips at this stage with the opening chapters. After working carefully through Chapter 7, he should briefly scan Chapters 8 and 9, and then proceed to Chapter 10, on 'The Working Day', which is, as we have already said, a highly readable chapter. We should also observe that it is extremely important for its *content*, and that it marks, in some respects, a climax in the book. The eleventh chapter, with its ingeniously abstract arguments, which are only 'simple' in a dialectical sense, should certainly be passed over for the present, and from the twelfth we should pick out only as much as is necessary to understand the quite lucid distinction Marx draws in the first few pages between 'absolute' and 'relative' surplus-value. This is the distinction between increasing the surplus labour expended for profit by means of the

absolute prolongation of the working day (Chapter 10), and increasing
surplus labour by relatively curtailing that proportion of labour-time
necessary to gain the subsistence of the worker himself, which is
achieved by means of a general increase in the productive capacity
of labour.

After this we move on to Chapters 13-15, which again were
recommended by Marx as particularly easy reading. These chapters
are easy, but in rather varying degrees. The simplest is the long
fifteenth chapter on 'Machinery and Modern Industry', which represents, both in form and content, a second climax of the work. The
thirteenth and fourteenth chapters, on the other hand, both present
greater conceptual difficulties. The fourteenth chapter in particular,
although it contains a few very simple passages, also introduces some
distinctions which are difficult and intricate at first sight. It is advisable to proceed from the first sections of this chapter, which discusses
the 'Two-fold Origin of Manufacture', straight to the fourth and fifth
sections, which deal with 'Division of Labour in Manufacture, and
Division of Labour in Society', and 'The Capitalistic Character of
Manufacture'.

By this time the reader has already come to a preliminary understanding of a large and crucial matter. He has become acquainted with
the actual process of *work and production,* the very heart of capitalism. It is now a matter of situating the process of work and production
in its surroundings, and in the general process of which it is one phase.
To this end we should turn next to Chapter 6 on 'Buying and Selling
of Labour-Power', and then to Part VI on 'Wages', leaving out
Chapter 22 on 'National Differences of Wages', which is rather difficult, even for the specialist, and reading for the moment just Chapters
19, 20 and 21.

The next step is Parts VII and VIII, which locates the process of
production in the uninterrupted flow of *reproduction and accumulation,*
that is in the continual process of self-perpetuation and self-develop-
ment – up to a certain limit – of the capitalist mode of production and
the bourgeois society that issues from it. Part VIII on 'The so-called
Primitive Accumulation' is again one of the portions of the book
which Marx recommended, as especially easy, for Frau Kugelmann
and is justly famous for its breath-taking pace and electrifying verve.
Besides being easy to read, this part which includes Chapter 33 on the
'Modern Theory of Colonisation', represents in an objective sense a
third climax of the book. But the reader who is prepared to work

eventually through the difficult parts as well as the simpler passages
of the book should save this part up until he really does come to the
end of Part VII, for Part VIII was intended by Marx as a final
crowning touch to his work.

There are a number of reasons why this is advisable. In the first
place the preceding chapters of Part VII may also be classed by and
large with the less arduous portions of the book, and so present no
special hinderance. Furthermore, the beginner who comes to the
chapter on 'Primitive Accumulation' too soon may well be misled into
thinking, along with Franz Oppenheimer and many others, that the
Marxian theory of primitive accumulation *is* the theory of *Capital*, or
at least its essential *basis*, whereas in fact it is merely one component
of the theory, indispensable but not predominant within it. It seems
advisable therefore to read Parts VII and VIII in the order in which
they stand, and then, having achieved a provisional grasp of the
general shape of the whole work, to proceed with a closer study of its
detail.

There are two points above all which must be elucidated if we are to
gain a deeper understanding of *Capital*. We have already touched upon
the first point in mentioning that mistaken estimate of the significance
of Part VIII in the overall theoretical framework of the book – a mis-
judgement that has wide currency both within and outside the Marxist
camp. It is not just a question of this part however, but also of a
number of other sections scattered throughout the book, and not developed into chapters in their own right. Among these passages are
the fourth section of Chapter 1, on the 'Fetishism of Commodities and
the Secret thereof', the third section of Chapter 9, on 'Senior's "Last
Hour" ', the sixth section of Chapter 15 on 'The Theory of Compen-
sation', and, perhaps most intimately connected with Part VIII on
'Primitive Accumulation', the two sections of Chapter 24 on the
'Erroneous Conception by Political Economy of Reproduction on a
Progressively Increasing Scale' and 'The So-Called Labour Fund'.

All these discussions, and a large number of other similar passages too, have this in common, that they represent a *critique* of
political economy – in a more specific sense than that in which the
whole work purports to be, as its sub-title declares, 'A Critique of
Political Economy'. The critical intention of these passages is immediately obvious from the kind of language they use, from their
explicit reference to the 'misconceptions' of individual economists (like

Senior) or of political economy as such, and from their description of the matter in hand as a 'secret' or as something 'so-called', masking something really quite different.

We may call these passages 'critical' then, in the narrower sense of the word, but on closer consideration we find that they in turn divide into two different types of rather unequal importance. The first type is that of ordinary academic criticism, where Marx, from his superior theoretical position, entertains himself and his readers with gleeful devastation of the aberrant quasi-scientific theories of post-classical bourgeois economists. To this category belong such passages as the brilliant demolition in Chapter 9 of the 'theory' of the well-known Oxford Professor Nassau Senior, on the importance of 'the last hour's work', and the refutation of another 'theory' discovered by the same 'earnest scholar' and still surviving today in bourgeois econo-mics, the 'theory' of the so-called 'abstinence' of capital. These parts of Marx's economic critique are among the most enjoyable passages in the book, and usually conceal beneath their satirical-polemical ex-terior a considerable fund of pertinent and significant insights, con-veyed to the reader in what we might call a 'playful' manner. Strictly speaking, however, these passages do not belong to the essential content of *Capital*: they might appropriately have been incorporated in the fourth book Marx projected, on the 'history of the theory', of which he wrote to Engels (31st July, 1865) that it was to have a more 'historical-literary' character in comparison with the theoretical parts (ie, the first three books), and that it would be the easiest part for him to write, since 'all the problems are solved in the first three books, and this last one is therefore more of a recapitulation in historical form'.

The second category of specifically 'critical' arguments in *Capital* are of a quite different kind. There are a considerable number of passages here which are less bulky but extremely important as regards their content. There is, for example, the delineation of that conflict over the limits of the working day, a conflict that cannot be resolved by reference to the laws of commodity exchange. Most important of all there is the final section of Chapter 1 on the 'Fetishism of Com-modities and the Secret thereof', and the final part of the whole work on 'The So-Called Primitive Accumulation' and the 'secret' it contains.

The Marxian 'Critique of Political Economy' begins, as an econ-omic theory, with the conceptual clarification of the real economic laws of motion and development of modern bourgeois-capitalist society.

This critique maintains the most scrupulous scientific consistency in order to follow through to their logical conclusion all the propositions advanced on this topic by the great economic theoreticians of the classical, ie revolutionary, period of bourgeois development, and concludes by exploding the very framework of these economic theories. Although in the section on the process of production and again, in the section on reproduction and accumulation, everything which can be said in economic terms about the origin of capital through surplus-value or unpaid labour is already stated, there still remains after all an unsolved problem to be elucidated, which proves in the last analysis, to be non-economic in character.

This problematic residue may be expressed in the following question: what was the origin, before all capitalist production began, of the first capital, and of the first relationship between the exploiting capitalist and the exploited wage-labourer? Already in the course of the economic analysis itself Marx had repeatedly pursued his line of enquiry almost to the point of posing this question – only to break off there each time; but now, in the final part of his work, he returns to this problem. First of all his critique destroys with merciless thoroughness the answer given to this 'ultimate question' of bourgeois economics not only by the straightforward champions of capitalist class-interests (Marx calls them the 'vulgar economists'), but also by such 'classical economists' as Adam Smith. Marx shows that theirs was not an 'economic' answer at all, but simply purported to be historical, and was in fact nothing more than legendary. Finally he addresses himself, with the same merciless and methodical realism to this 'economically' unsolved and still open-ended question. He too proposes not an economic, but an *historical* answer – although in the last analysis his solution is not a theoretical one at all, but rather a *practical* one that infers from past and present history a developmental tendency projecting into the future. It is only when we appreciate clearly the way in which Marx deals with the question of 'Primitive Accumulation' that we can understand the proper relation of this final part to the foregoing parts of his book, and also the position within Part VIII of the penultimate chapter, which concludes the historical examination of the origin and development of the accumulation of capital with a treatment of the 'Historical Tendency of Capitalist Accumulation'. These considerations also make clear the compelling methodological reasons why 'The So-Called Primitive Accumulation' belongs at the end, and not at the beginning or in the middle of *Capital*. It was for these reasons that

Marx positioned it there, and, for the same reasons, the reader too should save it up until the end.

The other point which has still to be elucidated, concerns not the connection between the individual sections and chapters, but the way in which the thoughts and concepts themselves are developed. It also concerns the few really grave difficulties raised by certain parts of Marx's work which we have not discussed yet – difficulties experienced not only by the untutored, but also by those who are at home in the subject, but are not philosophically trained. It is these difficulties that are chiefly responsible for the oft-reiterated complaint about the 'obscurity of *Capital*'. The passages in question are, above all, the third section of the first chapter on the 'Form of Value', which we have already mentioned briefly, and one or two passages closely connected with it in Chapter 3, dealing with 'Money'. Then there are a few other, rather less difficult parts, among them Chapters 9, 11 and 12, which we have also mentioned before, considered now in their proper relation to Chapters 16 to 18 on 'Absolute and Relative Surplus Value', which are often regarded superficially as a simple recapitulation of Chapters 9, 11, and 12. All these difficulties are integrally bound up with what is called the 'dialectical method'.

The explanation Marx himself gave (in the 'Afterword to the second German Edition') of the importance of this method for the structure and exposition of *Capital*, has often been misconstrued – whether honestly or not – to mean simply that in the formulation of his work, and in particular of the chapter on the theory of value, Marx 'flirted here and there' with the peculiar mode of expression of the Hegelian dialectic. When we look closer however, we recognise that even the explanation given by Marx himself goes much further than that. It implies in fact that he fully espoused the rational kernel (if not the mystical shell) of the dialectical method. For all the empirical stringency which Marx, as a scientific investigator brought to his observation of the concrete reality of socio-economic and historical facts, the reader who lacks a strict philosophical training will still find the very simple concepts of commodity, value, and form of value, rather schematic, abstract, and unreal at first sight. Yet these concepts are supposed to anticipate entirely, to contain within themselves, like a germ as yet undeveloped, the concrete reality of the whole process of being and becoming, genesis, development, and decline of the present-day mode of production and social order – and the concepts do indeed anticipate these realities. It is only that the connection is obscure or even invisible to the common eye. But the one who *is* aware of the connection, the author himself, the 'demiurge' who has re-created reality in the form of these concepts, refuses to betray the secret of his knowledge at the outset.

This is true above all of the concept of 'value'. It is well known that Marx invented neither the idea nor the expression, but took it ready-made from classical bourgeois economics, especially from Ricardo and Smith. But he treated the concept critically, and applied it, with a realism quite untypical of the classical political economists, to the actually given and changing reality around him. For Marx, in contrast with even Ricardo, the socio-historical reality of the relations expressed in this concept, is an indubitable and palpable fact.

'The unfortunate fellow does not see,' wrote Marx in 1868, about a critic of his concept of value, 'that, even if there were no chapter on "value" in my book, the analysis of the real relationships which I give would contain the proof and demonstration of the real value relation. The nonsense about the necessity of proving the concept of value arises from complete ignorance both of the subject dealt with and of the method of science. Every child knows that a country which ceased to work, I will not say for a year, but for a few weeks, would die. Every child knows, too, that the mass of products corresponding to the different needs require different and quantitatively determined masses of the total labour of society. That this necessity of distributing social labour in definite proportions cannot be done away with by the *particular form* of social production, but can only change the *form it assumes* is self-evident. No natural laws can be done away with. What can change, in changing historical circumstances, is the *form* in which these laws operate. And the forms in which this proportional division of labour operates, in a state of society where the interconnection of social labour is manifested in the *private exchange* of the individual products of labour, is precisely the *exchange-value* of these products.'

Compare this passage, however, with the first few pages of *Capital*, and consider what immediate impression these pages make on the reader who knows nothing as yet of the realistic 'background' to the author's arguments. Initially, it is true, there are a number of concepts introduced here which are taken from the 'phenomenal' realm, from the experience of certain facts about capitalist production. Among these concepts is the one that expresses the quantitative relationship of various kinds of 'use-values' being exchanged for one another, the idea, that is, of 'exchange-value'. This empirically-coloured notion of the contingent exchange relations of use-values promptly gives way however, to something quite new, arrived at by abstraction from the use-values of the commodities, something which only *appears* in the 'exchange relationship' of commodities, or in their exchange-value. It is this 'immanent' or inner 'value', arrived at by disregarding the phenomenon, which forms the conceptual starting point for all the subsequent deductions in *Capital*. 'The progress of our investigation,' declares Marx explicitly, 'will show that exchange-value is the only form in which the value of commodities can manifest itself or be expressed. For the present, however, we have to consider the nature of value independently of this, its form.'

Even when this progression is followed through we are not returned to anything like an empirical, immediately given phenomenon. We move instead, through an absolute masterpiece of dialectical conceptual development unsurpassed even by Hegel, from the 'Form of Value' to the 'Money Form', and then proceed to the brilliant, and, for the uninitiated, correspondingly difficult, section on the 'Fetishism of Commodities and the Secret thereof'. Only here do we learn that 'value' itself, unlike the corporeal commodities and the corporeal owners of commodities, is not something physically real, nor does it express, like the term 'use-value', a simple relationship between an available or manufactured object and a human need. 'Value' reveals itself instead as an 'inter-personal relationship concealed beneath a reified exterior', a kind of relationship integral to a definite historical mode of production and form of society. It was unknown, in this obscured and reified form, to all previous historical epochs, modes of production, and forms of society, and it will be just as superfluous in the future to societies and modes of production no longer based on producing commodities.

This example illustrates the *structure* of Marx's descriptions of things. Not only has that structure the intellectual and æsthetic advantage of an overwhelming force and insistence; it is also eminently suited to a science that does not subserve the preservation and further development of the present-day capitalist economic and social order, but is aimed instead at its subversion in the course of struggle and its revolutionary overthrow. The reader of *Capital* is not given a single moment for the restful contemplation of immediately given realities and connections; everywhere the Marxian mode of presentation points to the immanent unrest in all existing things. This method, in short, demonstrates its decisive superiority over all other approaches to the understanding of history and society in that it 'includes in its comprehension and affirmative recognition of the existing state of things, at the same time also, the recognition of the negation of that state, of its inevitable breaking up; it regards every historically developed form as in fluid movement, and therefore takes into account its transient nature not less than its momentary existence; it lets nothing impose upon it, and is in its essence critical and revolutionary'.

Anyone who wants to derive from his reading of *Capital* not just a few glimpses of the workings and development of modern society, but the whole of the theory contained in the book, will have to come to terms with this essential characteristic of Marx's mode of presentation. We should be deceiving ourselves if we were to think we could find a less strenuous access to *Capital* by reading it, so to speak, 'backwards' rather than from beginning to end. Not that it would be impossible to read it like that. If we did, we should certainly be spared, for example, the trouble of coming to grips in Chapter 11 with a number of laws concerning the relation between 'Rate and Mass of Surplus-Value', all of which are valid only if we disregard the possibility of 'Relative Surplus-Value' – which is not even raised until the *next* chapter. We should be spared the discovery in Chapter 16 *after* working through a similarly 'abstracted' treatment of the laws of relative surplus-value in the preceding chapters, that 'from one standpoint any distinction between absolute and relative surplus-value appears illusory' inasmuch as it transpires that 'relative surplus-value is absolute, and absolute surplus-value is relative'; and the discovery then that both categories in fact merely represent abstract elements of real, concrete surplus-value, – which reveals itself in turn as nothing more than one, highly abstract factor in the overall descriptive development leading up towards the actual phenomena of the economic reality around us.

All this we could avoid. But it is precisely upon this stringent method that the formal superiority of the Marxian analysis depends. It is a method which leaves nothing out of account, but which refuses to accept things uncritically on the strength of a superficial common-or-garden empiricism soaked in prejudice. If we cancel out this feature of *Capital* we are left in fact with the quite unscientific perspective of the 'vulgar economics' Marx so bitterly derided. Vulgar economics 'theorises' by consistently invoking appearances against the laws that underlie them, and seems in practice only to defend the interests of that class whose power is ensconced in the immediately given reality of the present moment.[2] It seems not to know, or not to want to know, that beneath the surface of this immediate reality there lies a profounder dimension, more difficult to grasp, but just as real; a dimension that embraces not only the given reality itself, but also its continual alteration, its origins, development and demise, its transition to new forms of life in the future, and the laws governing all these changes and developments. It may well be advisable all the same, even for the reader who is prepared in principle to submit to the dialectical progression of the argument in *Capital*, to scan a few pages of Chapter 16 before reading Chapter 11. This will reveal in advance something of the tendency of the argument in Chapter 11, a tendency we find on closer inspection to have begun much earlier even than this.

We have adduced a number of examples to illustrate the 'dialectical' relationship between an initially rather abstract treatment of a given object or nexus, and the subsequent, increasingly concrete, treatment of the self-same phenomenon. This mode of development, which characterises the whole structure of Marx's *Capital*, seems to reverse, or to 'stand on its head' the order in which given realities are 'naturally' regarded by the non-scientific observer. There is, as Marx declares repeatedly, no concept of wages in his analysis before the nineteenth chapter; there is only the concept of the value (and sometimes the price) of the 'commodity labour-power'. Not until Chapter 19 is the new concept of 'wages', which 'appears on the surface of bourgeois society as the price of labour', 'deduced' from the preparatory concept.

This dialectical mode of presentation is also connected with something else which the dialectically uninitiated (in other words the vast majority of present-day readers, whatever their academic qualification) find difficult to understand at first. This is Marx's use, throughout *Capital* and in his other works too, of the concept and principle of 'contradiction', especially the contradiction between what is called 'essence' and what is called 'appearance'. 'All science,' said Marx, 'would be superfluous if the outward appearance of things coincided exactly with their essence.' The reader will have to get used to this basic principle of Marxian science. He will have to get used to the sort of comment that is often made in *Capital*, to the effect that this or that 'contradiction' shown to be present in some concept, or law, or principle (in, for example, the concept of 'variable capital'), does not

2 One line of the German text has been jumbled at this point. I have supplied a probable reading by inference from the immediate context – *trans.*

invalidate the use of the concept, but merely 'expresses a contradiction inherent in capitalist production'. In many such cases a closer inspection reveals that the alleged 'contradiction' is not really a contradiction at all, but is made to seem so by a symbolically abbreviated, or otherwise misleading, mode of expression; in the case we have just mentioned of 'variable capital' this is pointed out by Marx himself. It is not always possible, however, to resolve the contradictions so simply. Where the contradiction endures, and the anti-dialectician persists in his objection to it, even as function of a strictly systematic logical-deductive treatment of concepts, then this opponent will have to be placated with Goethe's remark on metaphorical usage, which Mehring refers to in his interesting study of Marx's style:

'Do not forbid me use of metaphor;
I could not else express my thoughts at all'

Marx employs the 'dialectical' device at many crucial junctures in his work – high-lighting, in this way, the real-life conflicts between social classes, or the contrast between the realities of social existence and the consciousness of men in society, or the contrast between a deep-going historical tendency and the more superficial, countervailing tendencies which compensate, or even over-compensate for it in the short-run. These tensions are all pictured as 'contradictions', and this can be thought of as a sophisticated kind of metaphorical usage, illuminating the profounder connections and inter-relation between things. Exactly the same could be said of that other dialectical concept of the 'conversion' of an idea, an object, or a relationship into its (dialectical) opposite, the conversion, for instance, of quantity into quality. This is not used so often as the concept of contradiction, but it occurs at a number of decisively important points.

A number of appendices are provided to assist the practical use of this edition of *Capital*. These include notes on English coins, weights and measures etc mentioned in the book. But in addition to these we have also included an appendix of great theoretical importance. This contains Marx's famous recapitulation of his political and economic studies and the general conclusions to which they had given rise, which appeared as the *Preface to the Critique of Political Economy* in 1859. This resumé provides a penetrating insight into Marx's development as a student of society and economics, and into the essential features of his materialist conception of history. This was the conception he had worked through to in the mid-forties, leaving behind both Hegelian philosophical idealism and revolutionary-democratic political idealism. From 1845 he worked with Engels towards the completely matured version of this theory which received provisional formulation in the *Preface* of 1859.

Here Marx explicitly confirms what is obvious anyway from the pages of *Capital*, that he did not remotely intend to turn his new principle into a general philosophical theory of history that would be imposed from the outside upon the actual pattern of historical events. The same can be said of Marx's conception of history as he himself said of his theory of value; that it was not meant to be a dogmatic principle but merely an original and more useful approach to the real, sensuous, practical world that presents itself to the active and reflective subject. Fifty years ago Marx parried certain mistaken conceptions about the method of *Capital*, entertained by the Russian sociologist and idealist Michailovsky, by explaining that *Capital*, and in particular the conclusions arrived at in Part VIII on Primitive Accumulation, was not intended as anything more than an historical outline of the origins and development of capitalism in Western Europe.

The theories propounded in *Capital* may be said to possess a more general validity only in the sense that any searching, empirical analysis of a given natural or social structure has a relevance transcending its particular subject matter. This is the only conception of truth compatible with the principles of a strictly empirical science. The present development of European and of a few non-European countries already demonstrates to some extent that *Capital* may justly claim to possess such validity. The future will confirm the rest.

Why I am a Marxist

Instead of discussing Marxism in general I propose to deal at once with some of the most effective points of Marxist theory and practice. Only such an approach conforms with the principle of Marxian thought. For the Marxist, there is no such thing as 'Marxism' in general any more than there is a 'democracy' in general, a 'dictatorship' in general or a 'state' in general. There is only a bourgeois state, a proletarian dictatorship or a fascist dictatorship, etc. And even these exist only at determinate stages of historical development, with corresponding historical characteristics, mainly economic, but conditioned also in part by geographical, traditional, and other factors. With the different levels of historical development, with the different environments of geographical distribution, with the well-known differences of creed and tendency among the various Marxist schools, there exist, both nationally and internationally, very different theoretical systems and practical movements which go by the name of Marxism. Instead of discussing the whole body of theoretical principles, points of view in analysis,

* Originally published in the (American) *Modern Quarterly*, Vol IX no 2, April 1935, pp 88-95. Part of a symposium with other contributions *Why I am Not a Marxist* by Alexander Goldenweiser, George Santayana and H G Wells, and *Why I am a Marxist* by Harold Laski.

methods of procedure, historical knowledge, and rules of practice which Marx and the Marxists for more than eighty years have derived from the experience of proletarian class struggles and welded together into a unified revolutionary theory and movement, I shall, therefore, try to single out those specific attitudes, propositions, and tendencies which can be usefully adopted as the guide to our thoughts and action today, here and now, under the given conditions which prevail in the year 1935 in Europe, in the U S A, in China, Japan, India, and in the new world of the U S S R.

In this way the question 'Why I am a Marxist' arises, primarily, for the proletariat, or rather the most developed and energetic sections of the proletarian class. It can be asked, also, for sections of the population which, like the declining strata of the middle-classes, the newly arisen group of managerial employees, the peasants and farmers, etc do not belong either to the ruling capitalist or to the proletarian class so-called but may associate themselves with the proletariat for the purpose of a common struggle. The question may even be raised for such parts of the bourgeoisie proper, whose very life is threatened by 'monopoly capitalism' or 'Fascism', and it certainly arises for the bourgeois ideologists who, under the pressure of the cumulative strains of declining capitalist society, are individually making their way toward the proletariat (scholars, artists, engineers, etc).

I shall now enumerate what seems to me the most essential points of Marxism in a condensed form:

1. All the propositions of Marxism, including those that are apparently general, are *specific*.

2. Marxism is not *positive* but *critical*.

3. Its subject-matter is not *existing* capitalist society in its affirmative state, but *declining* capitalist society as revealed in the demonstrably operative tendencies of its breaking-up and decay.

4. Its primary purpose is not *contemplative enjoyment* of the existing world but its active transformation (*praktische Umwaelzung*).

I

None of these characters of Marxism has been adequately recognised or applied by the majority of Marxists. Again and again so-called 'orthodox' Marxists have relapsed into the 'abstract' and 'metaphysical' way of thinking which Marx himself – after Hegel – had most emphatically denied, and which indeed has been utterly refuted by the whole evolution of modern thought during the last hundred years. Thus, eg a recent English Marxist has once more tried to 'save' Marxism from the charges made by Bernstein and others to the effect that the course of modern history deviates from the scheme of development laid down by Marx, with the miserable evasion that Marx attempted to discover 'the general laws of social change, not only from the study of society in the nineteenth century, but also from a study of social development from the beginnings of human society', and that it is therefore *'quite possible'* that his conclusions are 'as true of the twentieth century as they were of the period in which he arrived at them'.[1] It is evident that such a defence destroys the true content of Marxian theory more effectively than the attacks made by any revisionist. Nevertheless this was the only answer given within the last thirty years by traditional Marxist 'orthodoxy' to the charges raised by the reformists that one or another part of Marxism was out of date.

For other reasons there is a tendency for the specific character of Marxism to be forgotten by the citizens of the Marxist Soviet State today who emphasise the general and universal validity of the fundamental Marxist propositions in order to canonize the doctrines underlying the present constiution of their state. Thus, one of the minor ideologists of present-day Stalinism, L Rudas, is trying to call into question in the name of Marxism the historical progress which was won by Marx ninety years ago when he accomplished the transposition (*Umstuelpung*) of the Hegelian idealistic dialectic into his materialistic dialectic. On the basis of a citation from Lenin which was used in an entirely different connection against the mechanistic materialism of Bukharin and which means something quite different from what Rudas says it means, the latter transforms the historical contradiction between 'productive forces', and 'productive relations' into a 'supra-historic' principle which will still apply in the remote future of the fully developed classless society. In the theory of Marx three fundamental oppositions are grasped as aspects of the concrete historical unity of the practical revolutionary movement. These are, in *economics*, the contradiction between 'productive forces' and 'productive relations'; in *history*, the struggle between social classes; in *logical thinking*, the opposition between thesis and antithesis. Of these three equally historical aspects of the revolutionary principle revealed by Marx in the very

1   A L Williams, *What is Marxism?* London, 1933, p 27.

nature of capitalist society, Rudas, in his supra-historical transfigura-
tion of the wholly historic conception of Marx, drops the middle term,
regards the *living conflict of the fighting classes* as a mere 'expression'
or result of a transitory historical form of the 'deeper lying' essential
contradiction, and retains as the sole foundation of the 'materialistic
dialectic', now inflated into an eternal law of cosmic development, the
opposition between *'productive forces'*, and *'productive relations'*. In so
doing he reaches the absurd conclusion that in present-day Soviet
economy, the fundamental contradiction of capitalist society exists in
'inverse' form. In Russia, he says, productive forces no longer rebel
against fixed productive relations but rather it is the relative backward-
ness of the productive forces in relation to the already achieved productive relations which 'drives forward the Soviet Union in an un-
precedently rapid tempo of development'.[2]

The contention set forth in my edition of Marx's *Capital* [3] that
all the propositions contained in this work, and especially those concerning 'Primitive Accumulation' as treated in the last chapter of the
book, represent only an historical outline of the rise and development
of capitalism in Western Europe and 'have universal validity beyond
that only in the same way in which every thorough empirical knowledge of natural and historical form applies to more than the individual
case considered', was unanimously rejected by spokesmen of both frac-
tions of German and Russian orthodox Marxism. As a matter of fact,
this contention of mine only repeats and emphasises a principle which
Marx himself fifty years ago had explicitly expressed in setting right
the idealistic Russian sociologist, Mikhailovsky, on his misconception
of the method of *Capital*. It is, indeed, a necessary implication of the
fundamental principle of empirical research which at our present time
is only denied by some inveterate metaphysicians. Compared to the

2   cf L Rudas, *Dialectical Materialism & Communism*, London 1934, pp 28,
29. 'Neither Marx, or Engels, nor Lenin ever said that the dialectical process
operates in society by the antagonism of classes . . . *Class antagonisms* . . .
are a driving force in class society because and only because they are *the
expression, the result* of the decisive contradiction of class society. . . . Once
this contradiction is eliminated . . . contradiction remains, but it takes another form. So for instance, in the Soviet Union . . . the Socialist productive
relations require a high level of productive forces, a higher one than the
Soviet Union inherited from capitalism. This is a contradiction which is
totally different, even inverse, to the contradiction existing in Capitalism, *but
it is a contradiction*. . . . Once, the highly developed productive forces re-
quired the development of social revolutions; in the future the higher social
relations will give room to the further development of the productive forces.'

3   Korsch's introduction is reprinted in this collection.

renaissance of this pseudo-philosophical dialectic in the writings of 'modern' Marxists, as exemplified in Rudas, how sober, clear and definite was the standpoint adopted by such old revolutionary Marxists as Rosa Luxemburg, and Franz Mehring who saw that the principle of materialistic dialectic as embodied in Marxian economics, means nothing more than the specific relation of all economic terms and propositions to *historically* determined objects.

All the hotly disputed questions in the field of *historical material-ism* – questions which when phrased in their general form are just as insoluble and just as meaningless as the well-known scholastic disputes about the priority of the hen or the egg – lose their mysterious and sterile character when they are expressed in a concrete, historical and specific manner. For example, Frederick Engels in his well-known letters on historical materialism, written after the death of Marx, out of undue consideration for the criticism of one-sidedness levelled by bourgeois and would-be Marxist critics against Marx's proposition that 'the economic structure of society constitutes the real foundation on which rise legal and political superstructures and to which correspond definite forms of social consciousness', actually modified Marx's doctrine. He unwisely conceded that to a large extent so-called 'reactions' (*Rückwirkungen*) might take place between the superstructure and the basis, between ideological development and economic and political development, thereby introducing completely unnecessary confusion into the foundations of the new revolutionary principle. For *without an exact quantitative determination* of 'how much' action and reaction takes place, without an *exact indication of the conditions* under which one or the other occurs, the whole Marxian theory of historical devel-opment of society, as interpreted by Engels, becomes useless even as a working hypothesis. As stated, it affords not the slightest clue as to whether one is to seek for the cause of any change in social life in the *action* (*Wirkung*) of the base upon the superstructure or in the *re-action* (*Rückwirkung*) of the superstructure upon the base. And the logic of the matter is not affected by such verbal evasions as 'primary' and 'secondary' factors, or by the classification of causes into 'prox-imate', 'mediate', and 'ultimate', ie those which prove decisive 'in the last analysis'. The entire problem disappears just as soon as we substi-tute for the general question of the effect of 'economics as such', upon 'politics as such', or 'law, art and culture as such', and vice versa, a *detailed description* of the definite relations which exist between defin-ite economic phenomena on a definite historical level of development and definite phenomena which appear simultaneously or subsequently in every other field of political, juristic and intellectual development. According to Marx, this is the way in which the problem is to be settled. His posthumuously published outline of a general introduction to his *Critique of Political Economy* – despite its sketchiness – is a clear and highly significant statement of the whole complex of problems. Most of the objections raised later against his materialistic principle are anticipated and answered. This is particularly true of the very subtle problem of the 'unequal·relation between the development of material production and artistic creation' which is evidenced in the well-known fact that 'certain periods of the highest development of art stand in no direct relation to the general development of society nor to the material basis of its organisation'. Marx shows the two-fold respect in which this unequal development takes definite historical form – 'the relationship between different forms of art within the domains of art itself' as well as the 'relationships between the whole field of art and the whole of social development'. '*The difficulty consists only in the general way these contradictions are expressed. Just as soon as they are made specific and concrete, they are therewith clarified.*'

II

As hotly disputed as my contention concerning the specific, historical and concrete character of all propositions, laws and principles of Marxian theory, including those that are apparently universal, is my second contention that Marxism is essentially *critical*, not positive. *The Marxian theory constitutes neither a positive materialistic philosophy nor a positive science.* From beginning to end, it is a theoretical as well as a practical *critique* of existing society. Of course the word 'critique' (*Kritik*) must be understood in the comprehensive and yet precise sense in which it was used in the pre-revolutionary forties of the last century by all left Hegelians, including Marx and Engels. It must not be confused with the connotation of the contemporary term 'criticism'. 'Critique' is to be understood not in a merely idealistic sense but as a materialistic critique. It includes from the point of view of the *object* an empirical investigation, 'conducted with the precision of natural science', of all its relations and development, and from the point of view of the *subject* an account of how the impotent wishes, intuitions and demands of individual subjects develop into an historically effective class power leading to 'revolutionary practice' (*Praxis*).

This critical tendency which plays such a predominant role in all

of the writings of Marx and Engels up to 1848 is still alive in the later
phases of development of Marxian theory. The economic work of their
later period is much more closely related to their previous philosophical and sociological writings than orthodox Marxist economists are inclined to admit. This appears from the very titles of their later and
earlier books. The first momentous work which was undertaken by
both friends in common as early as 1846 to present the opposition of
their political and philosophical views to those of contemporary left-
Hegelian idealism, carried the title *Critique of German Ideology*. And
in 1859, when Marx published the first part of his planned comprehensive economic work, as if to emphasise its critical character, he
entitled it *A Critique of Political Economy*. This was retained as a
subtitle of his chief work, *Capital: A Critique of Political Economy*.
Latter day 'orthodox' Marxists either forgot or denied the supremacy
of the critical tendency in Marxism. At best they regarded it as of
purely extrinsic significance and quite irrelevant to the 'scientific'
character of the Marxist propositions especially in the field which
according to them was the basic science of Marxism, viz economics.
The crassest expression which this revision took is to be found in the
well-known *Finanzkapital* of the Austrian Marxist, Rudolf Hilferding
which deals with the economic theory of Marxism as a mere phase in
the unbroken continuity of economic theory, entirely separated from
the Socialist aims and, indeed, with no implications for practice. After
having formally stated that the economic as well as the political theory
of Marxism is '*free from judgments of value*', the author points out
that 'it is, therefore, false to conceive, as is widely done, *intra et extra
muros*, that Marxism and Socialism are as such identical. For logically,
regarded as a scientific system and apart from its historical effect,
Marxism is only a theory of the laws of movement of society formulated in general terms by the Marxian conception of history, the Marxian economics applying in particular to the period of commodity-
producing society. But insight into the validity of Marxism which includes insight into the necessity of Socialism is by no means a matter
of value judgments and just as little an indication to practical procedure. For it is one thing to recognise a necessity, and another thing
to work for this necessity. It is quite possible for someone convinced of
the final victory of Socialism to fight against it.' [4]

4   cf Rudolf Hilferding, *Das Finanzkapital*, Vienna 1909, pp V I I - I X. The
quotations are taken from the English translation by Sidney Hook in *Towards
the Understanding of Karl Marx*. (English edition p 34; American edition p 27)

It is true that this superficial pseudo-scientific interpretation of orthodox Marxism has been opposed more or less effectively by contemporary Marxian theories. While in Germany the critical, ie revolutionary, principle of Marxism was openly attacked by the Bernstein revisionists and only half-heartedly defended by such 'orthodoxists' as Kautsky and Hilferding, in France the short-lived movement of 'Revolutionary Syndicalism', as expounded by Georges Sorel, tried hard to revive just this aspect of Marxian thought as one of the basic elements of a new revolutionary theory of proletarian class war. And a more effective step in the same direction was taken by Lenin who applied the revolutionary principle of Marxism to the practice of the Russian Revolution, and at the same time achieved a hardly less important result within the theoretical field by restoring some of the most powerful revolutionary teachings of Marx.

But neither Sorel, the Syndicalist, nor Lenin, the Communist, utilised the full force and impact of the original Marxian 'critique'. Sorel's irrationalist device by which he transformed several important Marxian doctrines into 'myths', despite his intentions, led to a kind of 'debunking' of these doctrines in so far as their practical bearing upon the revolutionary proletarian class-struggle was concerned, and ideologically prepared the way for the Fascism of Mussolini. Lenin's somewhat crude division of the propositions of philosophy, economics, etc into those which are *'useful'* or *'harmful'* to the proletariat (a result of his too exclusive concern with the immediate present effects of accepting or denying them, and his too little consideration of their possible future and ultimate effects) introduced that coagulation of Marxist theory, that decline and, in part, a distortion of revolutionary Marxism, which renders it very difficult for present-day Soviet-Marxism to make any headway outside the boundaries of its own authoritarian domain. As a matter of fact the revolutionary proletariat cannot, in its practical fight, dispense with the distinction between *true* and *false* scientific propositions. Just as the *capitalist* as a practical man, 'though he does not always consider what he says outside of his business yet in his business knows what he is about' (Marx), and just as the *technician* in constructing an engine must have exact knowledge of at least some physical laws, so must the *proletariat* possess a sufficiently true knowledge in economic, political and other objective matters in order to carry the revolutionary class struggle to a successful consummation. In this sense and within these limits the *critical* principle of materialistic, revolutionary Marxism includes strict, empirically verifiable knowledge, marked by 'all the precision of natural science', of the economic laws of the movement and development of capitalist society and the proletarian class struggle.

III

Marxist 'theory' does not strive to achieve objective knowledge of reality out of an independent, theoretical interest. It is driven to acquire this knowledge by the practical necessities of struggle, and can neglect it only by running the heavy risk of failing to achieve its goal, at the price of the defeat and eclipse of the proletarian movement which it represents. And just because it never loses sight of its practical purpose, it eschews every attempt to force all experience into the design of a monistic construction of the universe in order to build a unified system of knowledge. Marxist theory is not interested in everything, nor is it interested to the same degree in all the objects of its interests. Its only concern is with those things which have some bearing upon its objectives, and with everything and every aspect of everything the more so as this particular thing or this particular aspect of a thing is related to its practical purposes.

Marxism, notwithstanding its unquestioned acceptance of the genetic *priority (Priorität)* of external nature to all historical and human events, is primarily interested only in the phenomena and interrelations of historical and social life. That is to say, it is primarily interested only in what, relative to the dimensions of cosmic development, occurs within a short period of time and in whose development it can enter as a practical, influential force. The failure to see this on the part of certain orthodox Communist party Marxists accounts for their strenuous attempts to claim the same superiority undoubtedly possessed by Marxian theory in the field of sociology, for those rather primitive and backward opinions which to this very day are retained by Marxian theorists in the field of natural science. By these unnecessary encroachments the Marxian theory is exposed to that well-known contempt which is bestowed on its 'scientific' character even by those contemporary natural scientists who as a whole are not unfriendly to Socialism. However, a less 'philosophical' and more progressive scientific interpretation of the very concept of the Marxian 'synthesis of sciences' has just begun to manifest itself among the more intelligent and responsible representatives of the contemporary Leninist-Marxist theory of science, whose utterances are about as different from those of Rudas and Co as the utterances of the Russian Soviet Government are from those of the non-Russian sections of the Communist International. Thus, for example, Professor V Asmus in his programmatic article emphasises that in addition to the 'objective and methodological community' of history and natural sciences there exists at the same time the 'peculiarity of the social-historical sciences which do not allow in principle the identification of their problems and methods with those of the natural sciences'.[5]

Even within the sphere of historical-social activity, Marxist research is in the main interested only in the particular mode of production underlying the present epoch of 'social-economic formation' (ökonomische Gesellschaftsformation), ie the system of capitalist commodity-production as the basis of the modern 'bourgeois society' (bürgerliche Gesellschaft) regarded in the process of its actual historical development.[6] In its inquiry into this specific sociological system it proceeds, on the one hand, more thoroughly than any other sociological theory in that it concerns itself preferably with economic foundations. On the other hand, it does not concern itself with all of the economical and sociological aspects of bourgeois society equally. It pays particular attention to the discrepancies, flaws, shortcomings, and maladjustments in its structure. It is not the so-called normal functioning of bourgeois society which concerns Marxism but rather what appears in its eyes as the really normal situation of this particular social system, viz the crisis. The Marxian critique of bourgeois economy and of the social system based upon it culminates in a critical analysis of its Krisenhaftigkeit, that is to say of the ever-growing tendency of the capitalist mode of production to assume all the characteristics of actual crisis even within the ascendant or recovery phases, indeed, through all the phases of the periodic cycle through which modern industry runs, and whose crowning point is the universal crisis. An astonishing blindness to this basic orientation of Marxist economics which is so clearly expressed everywhere in Marx's writings, has led some recent English Marxists to discover a 'lacuna of some importance' in Marx's work, in his failure to establish the economic

5 Marxism and the Synthesis of Sciences in Socialist Construction in the USSR, published by V O K S, vol 5, 1933, p 11.
6 In its later phases it also considered certain social phenomenon of primitive society in order to draw some analogies between primitive Communism (Urkommunismus) and the classless communist society of a remote future.

necessity of recovery from crises after he had demonstrated the necessity of their rise.[7]

Even in the non-economic spheres of political superstructure and general ideology of modern society, Marxist theory concerns itself primarily with observable rifts and fissures, the strained splitting points which reveal to the revolutionary proletariat those crucial places in the social structure where its own practical activity can be most effectively applied.

In our day everything appears to be pregnant with its opposite. Machinery which is endowed with the most remarkable powers to shorten human labour and render it more productive has produced instead hunger and overwork. The new springs of wealth have become transformed by a peculiar magic formula of destiny into sources of poverty. The conquests of the arts seem to be won at the price of loss of character. To the extent that man controls nature he seems to be controlled by other men or by his own meanness. Even the pure light of science can apparently only shine against the dark background of ignorance. All our discoveries and progress seem to have had no other consequences than to endow material forces with spiritual life and to brutalise human life into a material force. This opposition between modern industry and science on the one hand, and modern poverty and decay on the other, this opposition between the productive forces and the social relations of our time is an obvious, overwhelming, undeniable fact. Some Parties may lament it, others may wish to get rid of modern proficiency and therewith of its conflicts. Or they may believe that such a remarkable progress in industry demands for its completion just as remarkable a retrogression in politics.[8]

IV

The specific features of Marxism so far discussed, together with the practical principle implied in all of them, which commands the Marxists to *subordinate all theoretical knowledge to the end of revolutionary action*, provide the fundamental characters of the Marxian *materialistic dialectic* on the basis of which it distinguishes itself from the idealistic dialectic of Hegel. The dialectic of Hegel, the bourgeois philosopher of the restoration, worked out to its finest details by him as an instrument of justification for the existing order with a moderate

7   cf R W Postgate, *Karl Marx*, London 1933, p 79, and the citations given by him from G D H Cole's *Guide Through World Chaos*, London 1932.

8   From a speech of Karl Marx delivered at the Fourth Annual Celebration of the Chartist *People's Paper*, April 14, 1856, printed in the issue of April 16. Translated from the German text in the *Vorwärts* of March 14, 1913.

allowance for a possible 'reasonable' progress, was *materialistically transformed* by Marx after careful critical analysis into a theory, *revolutionary not only in content but also in method*. As transformed and applied by Marx, dialectic proved that the 'reasonableness' of existing reality asserted by Hegel on idealistic grounds had only a transitory rationality, which in the course of its development necessarily resulted in 'unreasonableness'. This unreasonable state of society will in due course be wholly destroyed by the new proletarian class which, by making the theory its own and using it as a weapon of its 'revolutionary practice', is attacking 'capitalistic unreason' at its root.

Because of this fundamental change in its character and application, *Marxian dialectic* which, as Marx justly points out, in its 'mystified' Hegelian form had become fashionable among bourgeois philosophers, has now become 'a scandal and abomination to bourgeoisdom and its doctrinaire professors', for

it includes in its comprehension and affirmative recognition of the existing state of things, at the same time also, the recognition of the negation of that state, of its inevitable breaking-up; it regards every historically developed social form as in fluid movement and therefore takes into account its transient nature not less than its momentary existence; it lets nothing impose upon it, and is in its essence critical and revolutionary.[9]

Just as all the particular critical, activistic, and revolutionary aspects of Marxism have been overlooked by most Marxists, so it has been with the whole character of the Marxian *materialistic dialectic*. Even the best among them have only partially restored its critical and revolutionary principle. In the face of the universality and thoroughness of the present world crisis and of the increasingly sharper proletarian class struggles which surpass in intensity and extent, all conflicts of the earlier phases of capitalist development, our task today is to give our revolutionary Marxian theory corresponding form and expression, and therewith to extend and actualise the revolutionary proletarian fight.

London, October 10, 1934   *(Translation revised by the author)*

---

9   Karl Marx, Preface to the second edition of *Capital*. Quoted from the English translation by Moore and Aveling, London 1889, p xxx-xxxi.

MONTHLY REVIEW

an independent socialist magazine
edited by Paul M. Sweezy and Harry Magdoff

Business Week: ". . . a brand of socialism that is thorough-going and tough-minded, drastic enough to provide the sharp break with the past that many left-wingers in the underdeveloped countries see as essential. At the same time they maintain a sturdy independence of both Moscow and Peking that appeals to neutralists. And their skill in manipulating the abstruse concepts of modern economics impresses would-be intellectuals. . . . Their analysis of the troubles of capitalism is just plausible enough to be disturbing."

Bertrand Russell: "Your journal has been of the greatest interest to me over a period of time. I am not a Marxist by any means as I have sought to show in critiques published in several books, but I recognize the power of much of your own analysis and where I disagree I find your journal valuable and of stimulating importance. I want to thank you for your work and to tell you of my appreciation of it."

The Wellesley Department of Economics: " . . . the leading Marxist intellectual (not Communist) economic journal published anywhere in the world, and is on our subscription list at the College library for good reasons."

Albert Einstein: "Clarity about the aims and problems of socialism is of greatest significance in our age of transition. . . . I consider the founding of this magazine to be an important public service." (In his article, "Why Socialism" in Vol. I, No. 1.)

DOMESTIC: $7 for one year, $12 for two years, $5 for one-year student subscription.

FOREIGN: $8 for one year, $14 for two years, $6 for one-year student subscription. (Subscription rates subject to change.)

116 West 14th Street, New York, New York 10011

Modern Reader Paperbacks